Solidified In God:

The Devil Is Defeated

Solidified In God:

The Devil Is Defeated
The Preacher's Life

Pastor Blondie Morris Williams

Xulon Press

Xulon Press Elite
2301 Lucien Way #415
Maitland, FL 32751
407.339.4217
www.xulonpress.com

Unless otherwise indicated, Scripture quotations taken from the Amplified Bible (AMP). Copyright © 1954, 1958, 1962, 1964, 1965, 1987 by The Lockman Foundation. Used by permission. All rights reserved.

Scripture quotations taken from the English Standard Version (ESV). Copyright © 2001 by Crossway, a publishing ministry of Good News Publishers. Used by permission. All rights reserved.

Scripture quotations taken from the King James Version (KJV)—public domain.

Scripture quotations taken from the Holy Bible, New International Version (NIV). Copyright © 1973, 1978, 1984, 2011 by Biblica, Inc.™. Used by permission. All rights reserved.

Scripture quotations taken from the New King James Version (NKJV). Copyright © 1982 by Thomas Nelson, Inc. Used by permission. All rights reserved.

Scripture quotations taken from the Living Bible (TLB). Copyright © 1971 by Tyndale House Foundation. Used by permission of Tyndale House Publishers Inc., Carol Stream, Illinois 60188. All rights reserved.

Printed in the United States of America.
Edited by Xulon Press.

ISBN-13: 9781545621233

Table of Contents

Table Of Contents

Dedication

I dedicate this book to Christians and non-Christians
everywhere in the world.

Acknowledgments

Inspired by the Holy Spirit

I would like to honor my Father God in Heaven for living within me and providing me with the boldness to preach and teach His unadulterated Word. Through this methodology, I anticipate encouraging, illuminating, and educating readers through biblical perceptions, so that Godly principles become profoundly rooted within their spirits and conscientiously transcribed upon the dining tables of their hearts. If we are to live an everlasting life in Heaven, it is imperative to comprehend precisely what the Spirit of God is saying to the church. Consequently, this provides us with the anointing to live acceptable lives and it gives us the ability to empower others to shine as beacons of lights in the midst of dark places.

In the love of Jesus,

Dr. Blondie Williams

Introduction

On December 28, 1967, God determined within Himself to grace this world with an amazing individual such as myself. From my mother's womb, I was a chosen vessel of God, prepared and designated to accomplish my Master's divine will. I must say I am truly an anointed woman of God who is blessed to have life. My belated mother was an extraordinary woman who desired to have children with her husband. Consequently, she became impregnated on five occurrences, but unexpectedly experienced five losses through either stillbirths or spontaneous abortions. The fetuses, by the way, were unhealthy males. Subsequent her husband and her continuously attempting to enlarge their family, God rewarded their determination by blessing them with five beautiful, healthy daughters.

I am eternally grateful to God for His divine favor. Moreover, my belated parents were committed and dedicated to loving and caring for their family throughout the years God allowed them upon this earth. Particularly, we were raised to love God and eschew evil. It is exceptional for parents to educate their children concerning biblical principles, such as mine did. This guarantees that they are learning about and incorporating the strongest weaponry available to Christians. The Word of God is advantageous in destroying every temptation or stumbling block the Devil, or the Mastermind of Destruction, positions within people's pathways. Likewise, the Word is paramount in instilling invaluable life changing information within their spirits to assist them with walking in obedience to His Word.

We must remember to follow God's directions and instructions.
He loves us and cares for us, and He will always shelter us
from distractions, deceptions, and contraptions of the Devil
~ Blondie Williams ~

As children of God, we must trust and believe God with our complete heart, and, regardless of what disadvantageous circumstances we encounter, never doubt God's capability of shielding and protecting us. It is imperative to remain cognizant of the actualization that Satan is a defeated foe who comes for no other reasons than to steal, kill, and destroy anything and anyone he could. This is why Christians are to establish a strong, powerful, anointed, and perpetual prayer life. The Bible says in Luke 18:1 that Christians should always pray. Prayer is communication to God, and through it, we are strengthened spiritually, causing us to become more susceptible to the Spirit of God. It blesses us with a grander spiritual intelligence. It provisions Saints of God with Holy boldness, and it is overall contributory toward our developing and strengthening our relationship with our Father.

"Prayer and faith are powerful implementations
which simultaneously and collaboratively work
to cause our prayer requests to materialize"
~ Blondie Williams ~

God pronounces that faith is the ingredient to receiving things anticipated and the evidence or assurance concerning things undetected. Otherwise exemplified: "Now faith is the substance of things hoped for, the evidence of things not seen" (Hebrews 11:1 KJV). Therefore, the manifestations of our anticipations are unleashed through not only asking God but also believing in Him unwaveringly. The Holy Bible encourages us to maintain confidence in God and to never depend upon our own understanding, but through acknowledging Him, He will direct our pathways (Proverbs 3:5-6). It is important for us to understand that God makes no mistakes; therefore, we are not accidents. We are examples of His exceptional craftsmanship, full of His Spirit, and drenched in His love. If it were not for God's kindness and grace, we could have been stillborn or spontaneously aborted. Obviously, a loving and merciful Father determined within Himself that we shall not die but live, and accomplish our Master's will. Be cognizant that whether you desire to be married, have biological children, be healed, secure employment, or graduate from college with highest distinction, it is through prayer and faith that your requests become manifestations.

I give God praise for His multitude of blessings and His immeasurable love. God graciously permissioned us life upon this Earth for His divine purpose; as children of God, it is indispensable for us to communicate with our Father to become knowledgeable of our life's purpose. Remember, God alone is the navigational system that leads and guides us throughout our lives, and He is the determining constituent as to where we spend eternity. Therefore, we should designate time everyday reading and studying our Bibles, singing, worshipping, and praying to God, in the name of His Son, Jesus, thanking Him in all things. The Bible encourages us to study the Word of God to become approved of Him and to demonstrate a joyful, praiseful, and thankful spirit. Nonetheless, maintaining a spiritual heart, mind, and lifestyle provision us with peace in God and an overflow of blessings. God promised us perfect peace if we continually meditate upon Him. This means we must surrender our minds to contemplating and reflecting upon Him, which permission His anointing to thoroughly saturate and permeate us.

This is significant in Christians becoming steadfast and immovable concerning biblical standards of living. The Word of God is the light of God and should be showcased throughout Christians' lives. This is possible subsequent God's Word becoming rooted within our spirits and transcribed upon the tablets of our hearts. It is consequential for us to perpetrate the characterizations of our Father. Luke 6:44 explicates that a tree is acknowledged by the fruit it generates (AMP). For this reason, we should allow God to rake through our lives gathering everything that does not epitomize Him to establish us upon a Holy foundation, plant productive seeds within us, and cultivate us so we grow and develop spiritually, and, in turn, embolden others to do likewise.

Preaching the Gospel of Jesus Christ throughout the world is what Christians are commissioned to do in order to enlarge the body of Christ. In other words, God, through our acceptance of His Son, Jesus, came to reside within us, thus providing Christians with the capability of effectively teaching and reaching sinners. The angels in Heaven rejoice when sinners become Christians. Therefore, we must be obedient disciples and make sure we preach the Apostles' doctrine to as many sinners as possible, for this is our greatest commission.

According to 1 Peter 3:20, there were only eight souls saved in the previous world: Noah; his sons Shem, Ham, and Japheth; his wife; and his sons' three wives. Satan was victorious because he won more souls than God. Nevertheless, in the New Testament, God promised He would win more souls than the Devil. Consequently, the new agreement or promise is definitely a newer and better covenant. As such, the authority to seek out and save sin-sick souls through preaching the Gospel of Jesus Christ was placed upon Christians, and it is our life-long mission.

Christian Living: The Spiritual Fruit of God

CHAPTER 1

Accepting Jesus as Lord and Savior is the most remarkable determination any individual can make concerning his or her life. It behooves everyone to comprehend that he or she will spend eternity in either Heaven or hell. Firstly, let us understand what eternity represents. Eternity is a representation of an immeasurable quantity of time, an infinitive timespan, or an endless duration of time. Acknowledging this realization that either of these destinations is where every individual will inhabit infinitely is enough to cause Christians and non-Christians to endeavor to overcome evil through demonstrating Christ-like practicalities. The Word of God encourages the children of God to present themselves as living sacrifices to

Him through Holy lifestyles. Therefore, having sacred communion with God and being conscientiously and faithfully devoted to Him enables the light of the living God to uninterruptedly illuminate the life of a child of God. When God's unconditional love is showcased towards others within a spirit of genuineness or truthfulness instead of pretentiousness, the light of God within us shines brightly. To function in contradiction of God's love is evil. It is written within God's Holy Word "He that loveth not knoweth not God; for God is love" (1 John 4:8).

The spirit of love is the foundation of all Christians because love is of God. Therefore, Christians' lifestyles should be testaments of their foundation and ordination in Him. Our Father's anointing is necessary for children of God to live fruitful lifestyles. God is a Spirit, and His Spirit represents nine fundamental fruits. The spiritual Fruit of God encompasses "love, joy, peace, longsuffering, gentleness, goodness, faith, meekness, and temperance" (Galatians 5:22-23). In addition, love is communicated through an individual's pragmatisms (activities) and experienced as his or her emotional feelings or sensitivities. Love is the life force of Christian living. God requires us to not give others lip service through unproductive words of "I love you," but through unpretentious deeds showing genuineness, truthfulness, and demonstrating a giving spirit (1 John 3:18, TLB). The spirit of love is the essence of God. In view of that, children of God's characterizations should unambiguously represent these fruits.

Now, let us gain a thorough comprehension of the fruit of the spirit.

The Fruit of Love: Again, God is the Spirit of love. To be precise, love is descriptive of unselfishness, genuineness, trustworthiness, patience, and benevolence regarding the well-being or good of others. For example, God's consideration for or Fatherly regard towards human beings, brotherly and sisterly affection toward themselves and their adoration concerning others, parents love for their children, friends love for each other, and romantic and orgasmic love between husbands and wives, to name a few. Even though, there are differentiations of love, love is, nonetheless, a powerful and indispensable mechanism. As stated previously, the fruit of love is paramount and is characteristically sweet. Therefore, walking in love is walking in God. For God is the seed of love. God's love is enormous, in that, while we were living in sin, He commissioned His Son, Jesus, to give up His life through death so that, precipitating the world's acceptance of Jesus, everyone would instantaneously receive His everlasting love and life (Romans 5:8 KJV, John 3:16). Furthermore, concerning the fruit of love, God explicated that although there is love throughout the world, there is no greater love demonstrated than a man giving up his life for his friends (John 15:13 KJV). I am speaking of Jesus' death, of course. This is a huge epitomization of the love of God.

Remember: Christians' lives must always be
reflections of the spirit of love
~ Blondie Williams ~

The Fruit of Joy is an emotion best illustrated when an individual experiences gladness or happiness. These emotions are manifested subsequent a person receiving something that he or she emphatically preferred. For example, if an individual petitioned and believed God for transportation, and he or she finally purchased his or desired automobile, the individual would then demonstrate inward and outward expressions of blissfulness or joyfulness. According to the Bible, Christians should celebrate when God does great things in their lives. Celebrations of joy might be manifested through feasting with family members and friends when a loved one graduates from college or gets married. In addition, singing, instrument playing, and dancing might be illustrated subsequent an inspiring testimonial.

Accordingly, Romans 12:15 remind us to rejoice with individuals that are rejoicing and praising God, for this motivates them to repetitively share their experiences with others. When Christians are experiencing the storms of life, it is necessary to begin rejoicing as well; it is the gift of praise that causes us to forget our problems and enter into the presence of God's anointing, thus becoming stronger Christians. The Bible pronounces that the joy of the Lord is our strength (Nehemiah 8:10). So, as we travel our life's journeys, remember that in order to advantageously weather any intemperate storm, you must praise God as though your prayers are already answered. Faith is manifested through this practicality. On the other hand, if you do not walk in faith, you will never please God. Doubt is categorically a sin before God, just as worrying is. We must become religiously and spiritually convinced that God has the capability of supplying our needs. Then suddenly, before you realize it, you have praised your way out of your adverse circumstances, and then consequentially your joy becomes full.

Realize that God gives us our individual challenges so we might experience the fullness of His joy.

The Fruit of Peace: The spirit of peace is differentiated as the spirit of tranquility. Tranquility means to live free from hostilities and disturbances. God is a peaceful spirit. As such, the spirit of hostility should be circumvented. Hostility encourages animosity between two or more individuals. This bitterness is stimulated within conflicts and oppositions concerning people's unique conceptualizations or their moral or ethical constitutions. Either way, a hostile spirit is an unfriendly attitude, and confrontational behaviors should not be named amongst Christians. This is why studying and applying the Word of God to our lives is invaluable. Tranquility or peace is indicative of humbleness and quietness, which means to be coolheaded and self-possessed. God's anointing provisions us with peaceful attitudes and Christ-like behaviors that assist us in living powerful and respectful lives that can only be maintained through the Holy Spirit. What is more, the peace of God is a qualitative characteristic Christians should always be clothed in. We are ambassadors for Christ; for this reason, portraying the spirit of peace is a requirement.

Let us make God proud by making peace not
breaking peace. The fruit of peace is secured
and maintained through meditating upon His
Word every day, and through exhibiting the
fruit of love and joy

The Fruit of Longsuffering: Longsuffering is a fruit that provisions Christians with exceptional capabilities to cope. For
illustration, longsuffering (or suffering for extended periods
of time) teaches us to patiently endure life's inconveniences;
whereas, complaining throughout such tribulations or hardships diminish spiritual integrity. These sufferings are permitted by God to test the extension of essence, importance, or
convenience that Christians are to the kingdom of God.

Remember, Saints of God, when we undergo longsuffering,
we should not go around expressing that we are frustrated, tor-
mented, or aggravated by the Devil. Troublesome times build
us to higher dimensions in God. Spending less time complaining
and more time praying is paramount in how we handle life's
deprivations. Longsuffering is a fruit of God's spirit; therefore,
manifesting the spirit of cheerfulness when experiencing longsuffering acknowledges the fact that Christians humbly,

submissively, and ungrudgingly surrender to a non-complaining spirit, which is spiritually mature.

"Remaining praiseful is an extraordinary
methodology to pushing past painful times"
~ Blondie Williams ~

The Fruit of Gentleness: Gentleness is characteristic of an individual with moderate behaviorisms or nonabrasive reflections. In other words, a gentleperson is rather kindhearted and tender-natured. This prototypical Christian upholds ornaments of grace and beauty. These embellishments are blessings from God to guarantee His children are elaborately furnished in Christian ornamentations. However, the fruit of gentleness is a stimulant for greatness, 2 Samuel 22:36 KJV elucidates that our salvation is both privileged and comprehensively sheltered by God, and our gentle nature distinguishes us as abundant in God's kingdom. It is indispensable for Saints of God to demonstrate the fruit of gentleness throughout life, for it is a remarkable reflection of the spirit of God. No individual within this lifecycle can ever become outstandingly accredited as good-looking or attention grabbing, spiritually, without the fruit of gentleness, along with the other forthcoming fruit of the spirit. Only the oil of God's anointing can garnish individuals with such character beautifications and transform them into great vessels of honor.

The Fruit of Goodness: This fruit is an exemplification of virtue, which means these individuals are differentiated as characteristically upstanding and morally decorous thus maintaining irreproachable or impeccable conduct. These comportments or approaches are ingredients that provoke an excellent disposition. It is through the wisdom of God that individuals are able to demonstrate intrinsic worth through virtues surrounding self-discipline, endurance, generosity, good judgment, assurance, and influence, for illustration. We must trust that God's anticipation is for His children to perform in correspondence with His Word. This propensity substantiates us as true children of God. In 2 Peter 1-8, God encourages us through faith in Him and Jesus, our Savior, to function within the spirit of virtue, for virtue is instrumental in sidestepping lustful worldly corruptions. The world's corruptions might manifest in briberies, financial embezzlements, fraudulent accomplishments, and supplementary unethical and criminal misappropriations.

Therefore, fuel your cognizance through the Holy Word of God so that your comportments are demonstrations of the heart of God.

The Fruit of Faith: The Holy Bible says in Hebrews 11:1 (KJV), "Now faith is the substance of things hoped for, the evidence of things not seen." As aforementioned, a doubtful Christian is a disbelieving Christian, and therefore cannot please God. When God's children approach Him, it is momentous for them to understand that believing in and steadfastly remaining in God guarantees them their requests. John 15:7 encourages us to abide in God and have full assurance that His promises will never become annulled but rewarded. The Spirit of God states: "If ye abide in me, and my words abide in you, ye shall ask what ye will, and it shall be done unto you" (John 15:7, KJV). This is our Father's promise to us; for this reason, we should never become double minded, but simplistically believe what He says. God is not a liar and He will never become a liar. What He promised, He will indisputably accomplish. Therefore, without question, whatever our recommendations incorporate, through faith, we shall have them.

The Fruit of Meekness: This fruit is consequential in Christians demonstrating submissiveness, meekness, and humbleness throughout life, especially toward God. Possessing such char-acterizations is profitable in the children of God withstanding or enduring disadvantageous provocations. The Bible emboldens us to hold up biblical standardizations when we encounter temptations. God permits us to experience temptations so our faith becomes strengthened. He reminds us that the trying of our faith works patience (James 1:3 KJV). Patience is virtuous and makes Christians honorable through exemplifying the spirit of meekness throughout their prosecutions and suffer-ings. Furthermore, perseverance and endurance is acceptable if we are to become blameless soldiers of Jesus.

However, humbleness and quietness are supplemental attri-butions of the fruit of meekness. Individuals that demonstrate the fruit of meekness fundamentally have teachable spirits. Psalm 25:9 (NIV) states God leads and guides the humble in appropriate judgment and teaches them to live within align-ment of biblical philosophies (ways of life). Likewise, God says in receiving and conforming to biblical teachings, "the meek will inherit the land and enjoy peace and prosperity" (Psalm 37:11). Therefore, remaining meek and humble when experiencing inflammatory provocations causes the light of God to illuminate us. True Christians, however, circumvent confrontations. The

Bible reminds us to persistently strive, which is symptomatic of becoming devoted to accomplishing a mission against all opposition, while manifesting nonviolent mannerisms. Fundamentally, the spirit of meekness is an essential embodiment of the nature of Christians.

The Fruit of Temperance: Temperance is phenomenal in equipping children of God with the ability to function in moderation. Whether throughout our thinking processes, performances, personal feelings, or conversations, it is indispensable for Christians to have self-refrainment and not become overindulgent. An overindulgence of anything is sinful. Self-refrainment is epitomized as having strength of mind or self-restraint, which is essential in Christians maintaining an honorable name and reputation before God and man.

Overindulging or disproportionately eating and drinking are gluttony, and motor mouths or overindulgent communicators are examples of immoderation. Because an overindulgence of anything is sinful, it is appropriate for Christians to demonstrate self-discipline or willpower, at all times, to successfully manage themselves, regardless of the circumstance. Comparative to the previous fruit, embracing the spirit of temperance strengthens the eminence of Christians. The collective fruit of the spirit is the personification of characteristics symbolizing the nature of God, and contribute to Christians' spiritual growth and development in their relationship with Him.

As we travel our spiritual journeys, we must thoughtfully and meticulously live a fruitful standard of living. In the midst of our struggles, however, we must understand we are imperfect beings and subject to mistakes. For this reason, it is advantageous for children of God to maintain themselves within Christian charisma; whereas, the aforementioned fruit is considerable in Christians controlling their temper during disadvantageous experiences and so maintaining the attractiveness of God's spirit. Our minds, hearts, and spirits must be without spots or wrinkles if we anticipate cleansing sinners through preaching the Gospel.

Let us remember, God is continuously
perfecting us characteristically to become the
grandest exemplifications of Him on this side
of Heaven ~ Blondie Williams ~

The True Vine: Baring the Fruit of God's Spirit

"I am the true vine, and my Father is the husbandman. Every branch in me that beareth not fruit he taketh away: and every branch that beareth fruit, he purgeth it, that it may bring forth more fruit. Now ye are clean through the word which I have spoken unto you. Abide in me, and I in you. As the branch cannot bear fruit of itself, except it abide in the vine; no more can ye, except ye abide in me. I am the vine, ye are the branches: He that abideth in me, and I in him, the same bringeth forth much fruit: for without me ye can do nothing" (John 15:1-5 KJV)

Standing Fast in Freedom: Grace and Mercy

CHAPTER 2

To experience true liberty in God, Christians must become knowledgeable of the importance of God's grace and mercy. We are saved by the faith of God through the grace of God. Salvation is not fleshly provided by people, but spiritually gifted to individuals from God. His grace is sufficient to everyone who believes.

Grace is understood as divine and unmerited assistance and advantage provided to Christians for their dedication and consecration to Him (Merriam-Webster, 2017). Correspondingly, sanctification means to be set apart or to become disconnected from uncleanliness so cleanliness might be established and enjoyed through the grace of God. God's grace empowers us with capabilities to conduct ourselves within polite characteristics. Mercy is demonstrated through God's spirit of compassion, kindness, and forgiveness. It is an extinguisher of people's atonements through showing pardon. Therefore, grace, through God's unmerited favor, must be accepted through faith previous to receiving restoration from insubordinations, for this is His grace. To live a triumphant lifestyle proceeding God's redemptive power is to endeavor to live a lifestyle that permissions one to honor the Word of God. This is an illustration of our love for God. This ornamentation gives Christians the aptitude and the altitude advantageous in living victoriously. The grace of God provisions Christians with the capability and mobility to function within God's Spirit. Because there are continuous conflictions between our spirit and our flesh, if, we as Christians, walked in alignment with God's Spirit, we can circumvent accomplishing fleshly or lustful passions.

While the Devil is unceasingly fighting for our minds, so is God. If the adversary takes authority over our minds, he has our bodies. Christians, we must become solidified in God, not halted between two opinions or straddling the fence, which is indicative of a double-tongued and double-minded person.

For example, consider those individuals who confess salvation today and live as sinners tomorrow. Demonstrating the fruit of God's Spirit is extraordinary in defeating the adversary and demolishing His weaponry. For this reason, as children of God, we must always dress ourselves in the complete armor of God, which prepares us for spiritual warfare. As soldiers in God's militia, we must not only fight, but also triumph over our adversaries. Victory is ours!

The Bible informs Christians that no ammunitions or weapons released by the Devil or his demons are prosperous, and judgmental conversations held pertaining to them are condemned. Nevertheless, we are to defend ourselves against Satan's weapons of attack through preparing our spirits, receiving powerful war clothes and shoes, and weapons of warfare that award children of God with spiritual expertise during spiritual confrontations or battles.

The Protection of God

The Protection of God is the facilitation of the armor of God that circumnavigates His given strategy for executing power and authority over Satan. The Protection of God is implemented through the strength of God within us. God is omniscient and comprehensively powerful. Therefore, because He maintains residency within our spirits, we are powerful men and women of God. Nevertheless, our lives are not designed to be perfect or troublesome-free, for God permissions Satan to launch attacks against us so that we might become deeply rooted or solidified in Him through our faith and dependency upon Him to bring us through bothersome times.

Implementing stratagems of defense is a necessity. For this reason, God prepares us through teaching and training us how to defeat our adversaries when fighting. He does this spiritually through us accepting the Lord as our personal Savior, characteristically through us demonstrating the fruit of the Spirit of God, psychosomatically through us keeping our minds set upon spiritual things, and strategically through methodologically employing a shield of protection around us and then subsequentially instigating a strategic technique to counterattacking the adversary.

Beforehand, protective armaments are representations of God's armor gear, and these defense mechanisms are provided to Christians during spiritual military operations or during hostilities between our adversaries. As Christian soldiers, we must remember our weaponry is not physically constructed by human beings, but are spiritually manipulated and executed in God for pulling down strongholds (2 Corinthians 10:4 NKJV). Whatever our battles encompass, it is beneficial to have successfully accomplished a spiritual training preparatory in order to strategically and competently assume these defensive armaments, acknowledged as the armor of God.

The Protective Armaments of God Explained

Ephesians 6:13-20 presents the first armament of God as a Belt of Truth. Christians are supposed to securely fasten themselves within truthful demonstrations and conversations. We should not bear false witness, but present everything truthfully. If information has not been substantiated as truth, do not communicate it to anyone. We should always show genuineness and trustworthiness.

The second armament is the Breastplate of Righteousness. This particular mechanism protects our chest, breast, and heart. Additionally, it is responsible for our emotional feelings and emotional recognizance. The breastplate also protects us from circumventing walking in the unconditional love of God as well as never demonstrating hate toward our adversaries. We are to love them as we love ourselves, yes, even when we are attacked, for God commissions this to us. Therefore, to live free from disobedience and guilt, we must abide within His Word. This typifies the spirit or fruit of righteousness; however, the breastplate is protection against unrighteousness. As the righteousness of God, in Christ, we are trusted by our Father to perform righteously and honorably.

Third, our feet must be adorned with spiritual footwear ordained by God to guarantee Christians' footsteps are effective in transcendentally preaching (throughout the world) the Gospel of peace. Christians are ordained and sent by God to preach the Gospel to save sinners. Preaching is to touch them spiritually through the love and compassion of God, which is demonstrated through His forgiving, accepting, and cleansing power. Ecclesiastical preachers or ministers are associated with having beautiful feet. Romans 10:15 states that beautiful are the feet of those who preach the Gospel of peace and bring tidings of gladness and goodness (TLB). Therefore, Christians are to adorn their feet in footwear, not for running toward mischievousness, but for walking within the Spirit of peace.

The fourth armament is the Shield of Faith. This ammunition is provided in defense of Satan's hateful attacks, through extinguishing every fiery missile He launches.

The fifth armament is the Helmet of Salvation. The helmet is worn throughout our salvation to safeguard Christians' heads from impact. As spiritual soldiers, this protective headpiece covers us psychologically to safeguard our spiritual intelligence. Satan's *modus operandi* (or method of operation) is fundamentally to destroy our minds. Satan is a deceiver and a destroyer. The Bible tells us that he comes for no other purpose. Consequently, if he can manipulate the minds of God's children to think upon evil things, he knows eventually he could manipulate our performances. Human beings' brainpower is responsible for generating dictations throughout their bodies. This is why accepting Jesus is imperious. A relationship with God, through His Son, Jesus, transforms our minds psychologically to integrate spiritual thoughts or meditations. Philippians 2:5 remind us we are to have the same spiritual mind as Christ Jesus. The fullness of joy is manifested when Christians become likeminded with Jesus, through demonstrating the same love of God, being in agreement, and having one mind (the mind of Christ). Overall, the helmet of salvation is germane in protecting

Christians while working collaboratively in one heart, in one mind, in one Spirit, and for one purpose, which is furthering the Gospel of Jesus Christ to persuade non-Christians to receive salvation through Him. We must show a genuine interest in the body of Christ and others, and maintain a consciousness to never perform in vainglory; in other words, not performing to impress others, but rather, to please God. The Bible says to "Let this mind be in you, which was also in Christ Jesus" (Philippians 2:5 KJV).

The sixth armament is the Sword of the Spirit. This ammunition is acknowledged as the Word of God, and it is the Gospel of our salvation. Moreover, it is a superlative defense that is prodigiously anointed. The Sword of the Spirit (the living Word) is particularized in Hebrews 4:12 TLB as God speaking in a vernacular that is full of living power. This means, according to Hebrews 4:12 that God's voice is full of life and are comprehensively powerful, thus making His word functional, motivational, and effectual. Otherwise stated, its operation is instantaneously responsive, commanding, and piercing more than any two-edged sword, well capable of penetrating between soul and spirit, and joint and marrow. Furthermore, it discerns and judges the contemplations and intentions of an individual's heart (KJV). This ammunition safeguards against filthiness, scandalous conversations, sexual promiscuities, drug utilization and addiction, prostitution, and supplementary performances that separate us from God. The moment we accepted the Word of God, the Sword carved out unfruitful desires from within our spirits. Therefore, speaking the Word is a weapon that puts the Devil on the run.

"Nothing can stand against the Word of God.
It is impossible for the Word to return void
or empty of accomplishing what we send it to
complete" ~ Blondie Williams

For illustration, if your adversary has a vendetta against your family, the Sword of the Spirit will cut down his weapons by you speaking authoritatively, with the power and the fire of the Holy Ghost, that no one can have you or any constituent of your family. With full assurance, speak in the name of Jesus, "My family is anointed and appointed by and dedicated to God!" For it is written: as for me and my household, we shall forever serve the Lord (Joshua 24:15 KJV). Therefore, no, Satan! You lose! You will not have ownership of me! You will never take guardianship of my husband! You will never become the proprietor of the mentalities of my children! We are not your property! Our hearts, minds, spirits, and bodies are faithfully and fanatically devoted to God for ministering the Gospel throughout the world, so get out of here forever, in the name of the Lord Jesus Christ!

The Word is purifying; whereas, the sharpness
of the Sword keeps Christians walking upon
a clean and clear pathway to Heaven, thus
permitting them to live powerful lives that
perpetrate the life of God's Word
~ Blondie Williams ~

Spiritual Overcomer and Transformer
CHAPTER 3

I overcame sin and became transformed in God early in life. One day, as a child, I remember watching and listening to a ministerial leader on Trinity Broadcasting Network (TBN) teaching and preaching the Word of God. I recollect, thoughtfully, concentrating upon the message and becoming moved and encouraged within my spirit. I comprehended the consequentialness of accepting Jesus as my personal Savior. Through accepting Jesus, my relationship with God became solidified, my transgressions were forgiven, I became cleansed, purified, sanctified, and filled with the Holy Spirit. Finally, my name was documented within the "Lamb's book of life" (Revelation 21:27) or journalized in Heaven as a transformed and redeemed child of God.

Throughout the years, I have continuously communicated with God, thus becoming a stronger Christian. Requesting for and trusting Him for a loving and God-fearing husband, effective communication, a dynamic and orgasmic sex life, children, financial stability, longevity, and to become a highly effective child of God. Traveling my life's journey, I endeavored to stimulate others biblically. At sixteen years of age, I individualistically read and studied the Word of God from Genesis to Revelation, through the Holy Spirit's ministration. I do not personally know of any young adult or older adult who has ever designated this amount of time studying God's Word. All I remember is the desire to know God for myself. As a young Christian, it was then, and it is now, my responsibility. We are all encouraged to live God-filled lives through denouncing sinful practicalities and accepting Jesus as our Lord and Savior.

As an ambassador for Christ, I have encountered my share of temptations as much as anyone. Accordingly, I became submissive to premarital sex on two occasions during my middle school years; this eliminated my desire to marry as a virgin. God embraced me in His arms of forgiveness, rehabilitating me and reestablishing me. Throughout high school, I remorselessly lived and breathed the existence of a redeemed Christian, standing fast on theological principles. Subsequent to this period of my life, I reverted to fornication.

However, God continued to forgive me though I struggled to walk uprightly before Him and the general population. During my first collegiate tenure, I met the man who would become my husband. Around ten years of age, God promised me a husband. In December 1987, we were introduced, and following our introduction and preliminary conversation, we strongly believed we had a future together. We communicated concerning marriage, family, and Christianity. Our connection was unmistakably from Heaven, and we acknowledged that God designated and foreordained us to espouse each other. In my spirit, my confidence was that we could have gotten married the same week. Concerned with what people would say regarding a minimal courtship, we procrastinated.

Once again, Satan sidetracked me. Procrastination can unquestionably lead to sin. These lustful and sinful escapades were not acceptable before God. This man would sing to me as we walked down Ft. Lauderdale beach, holding hands and looking deeply into each other's eyes. He was a romantic, and we fell in love rather quickly. Howbeit, our preordainment to become espoused is no excuse to sin. The Bible says in 1 Corinthians 7:9 KJV, "if they cannot contain themselves, it is better for a man and woman to become married, than it is for them to burn in sexual yearning for each other." Momentarily, praise God, we were married. As a consequence, He honored our marriage and anointed our bed. My husband and I rededicated our lives to God, joined a church, grew further in the knowledge of Him, continued living according to biblical philosophies, and then we were ordained as deacon and deaconess. We continued to live as Saints of God, thereafter. It is understood that in this fleshly body, Christians are capable of sinning; therefore, we must become watchful, prayerful, and permanently dressed in the armor of God. This protection is prerequisite in defending ourselves against Satan and His temptations. We must also make certain that our spiritual ears are fine-tuned so we can unmistakably hear the voice of God, and move to action when He speaks.

Nevertheless, I thank God for being able to broadcast that previous to my husband's passing, he had no curable or incurable STDs, neither HIV nor AIDS, and I do not have either of those contaminations to date. I thank him for protecting us.

God is definitely an amazing Father. I truly love and honor Him with my whole heart.

Unpretentiously, my confession before the world is that I am solidified in God, and therefore, the Devil is defeated. So, regardless of what problematical experiences you encounter, whether you are ridiculed or laughed at, referenced as incompetent, or sexually assaulted, as I was, you must endure hardships as strong and powerful Christians. We must always remain confident that God's Spirit will both comfort and strengthen us throughout disparaging experiences. I love myself and I am encouraged through acknowledging the fact that God loves me. According to Psalm 139:14, I am fearfully and wonderfully sculptured KJV, I am not incompetent but intelligent, and I am blessed and favored of God. These are motivating connotations I tell myself to remind me to see myself as God sees me. Regardless of who does not appreciate me or celebrate me, I cannot be prohibited. I have always been accomplished, for I trust my Father in all things and at all times. I was co-captain of a cheerleading squad, undefeated in both of my school track and field events (shot-put and discus throws), and, at a banquet held for high athletic performers, I had the pleasure of meeting Robert "Bob" Beamon, an outstanding Olympian and United

States Olympic Hall of Fame inductee. I experienced some of my proudest moments during this time span. What was fascinating was my track and field coach, Coach Hall, offered me an opportunity to train for the 1986 Olympics. Unfortunately, my father did not give me permission to take advantage of this opportunity.

Furthermore, I am a seven time collegiate graduate with five honorary commendations. I accomplished my MBA with a 4.0 GPA. I began a Doctor of Business Administration DBA program, and, at the time of this writing, I have a 4.0 GPA. I know I shocked the Devil and his demons when my average was announced. Incompetent? Never! I might have heard this throughout my life, but the Devil is a defeated foe. I am highly intellectual, and I give my Father God all the praise.

Additionally, my spiritual ordainments incorporate spiritual novelist, evangelist, and prophetess. As of 2015, I became an ordained pastor through the United National Church in Atlanta, Georgia. I was delivered from immorality and became transformed in God, and so can you. The armor of God is instrumental in defending against hell's temptations, rejecting Satan's discouragements, and, in turn, unswervingly living a spiritually fruitful lifestyle while uninterruptedly teaching others to do the same. Demonstrating the fruit of the Spirit, as presented and described previously, has been my purpose throughout every constituent of my life, subsequent to undergoing my spiritual rehabilitation. I appreciate my Father for providing me with a belt to gird my loins when in battle with the adversary and a spiritual belt providing me protection by buckling up my bottom garment so my abdominal and pubic regions do not become visible or assessable, which contribute to circumventing sexual sins and remaining acceptable before God. Either way, to gird up your loins is representative of being spiritually conditioned to overcome challenging tasks, which is substantial in honestly presenting your bodies as sacrificial offerings to God.

For instance, in January 2013, my husband was injured at work. He was tying down a load of steel and slipped off the truck, landing on his back. He was rushed to the hospital, and it was reported that his skull was fractured, which caused his brain to swell. The physicians tried everything, yet they failed at reducing and stopping the swelling. In consequence, my husband was disconnected from the ventilator and pronounced dead. I am grateful to God for helping me and keeping me strong through this difficult time. It has been four years and nine months since my husband passed, and I have not engaged in any premarital sexual relationships, participated in masturbation, or played with sexual toys. I persevere through standing strong in faith employing the armaments of God. I am astronomically thankful and praiseful to Him for this victory over the enemy. I live a sin-free lifestyle and I am psychologically healthy. Praise the Lord!

When going through hardships, my breastplate of righteousness safeguarded my bosom, the centralized compartment where my emotions, feelings, and thoughts are established. Wearing it throughout the years has enabled me to focus upon God, His love, and His goodness. My spiritual helmet has been imperative to my fight in maintaining spiritual and wholesome thoughts; it has been momentous in assisting me with performing righteously. Furthermore, entertaining impure thoughts is one of Satan's contrivances or deceptions implemented as a methodology of separating us from God, so we would backslide into an environment of immoral involvements. Contemporaneously, I am traveling through life wearing shoes of peace and preaching the Word of peace; holding my powerful shield of faith as a methodological defense apparatus that protects me from Satan's destruction; and carrying a sharp sword (the unadulterated Word of God) to instantaneously pull out and slice away every spiritual principality and demonized force that come neigh my dwelling. Implementation of this ammunition is functional in my advantageously weathering the storms of life. This caused me, as a Saint of God, to circumnavigate transgressions, fight diligently to maintain a close and an intimate relationship with God, preach God's word continually to maintain spiritual transformation, and endeavor to transform the hearts, minds, and spirits of non-Christians unto God.

Solidified in God by His Spirit
CHAPTER 4

The true Word of God solidifies our salvation in God through solidifying the promise of filling us with the Holy Ghost. The Holy Ghost is additionally epitomized as the Holy Spirit. The Holy Spirit is our teacher, and He is responsible for teaching and ministering biblical truths to the spirit of Christians and reminding us of everything God promised. John 14:26 elaborates: "But the comforter, which is the Holy Ghost, whom the Father will send in my name, he shall teach you all things, and bring all things to your remembrance, whatsoever I said unto you" (KJV).

Ephesians 1:3 states that our salvation is solidified and we are blessed with every spiritual blessing KJV. This means believers were elected before the foundation of the world, predestinated and adopted by Jesus, redeemed from sin by accepting Him, distributed spiritual competence and prudence (comprehension), established with a spiritual inheritance, solidified or sealed by the Holy Spirit, entered into the newness of life, and given citizenship in God through His grace.

Correspondingly, it is important for Christians to comprehend there are three spiritual influences that dwell within them, the Trinity: The Father (first person, God), the Son (second person, Jesus), and the Holy Ghost (third person, the Spirit of God). These are orchestrated and demonstrated through the same spirit and formalized into one spirit. This empowerment is solidified within the spirits of Christians, and is an enablement to advocating and showcasing Christ-like characterizations, as aforementioned. What is more, through God's authorization, Christians are given spiritual authority to meaningfully and significantly accomplish the ecclesiastical work of the Lord. God stimulates saints by equipping us and qualifying us to perform duplicate works as Jesus, and even greater accomplishments shall we achieve. For this reason, saints must be attentive to investigating and studying this spiritual phenomenon and never hesitate to speak the Word of God exclusively. In consequence, our spiritual consciousness or awareness becomes strengthened throughout our Christian responsibilities.

Joy in the Holy Spirit

Once we are filled with the Holy Spirit, we experience true joy in the Holy Ghost. Ecclesiastically speaking, Christianity and spirituality belong to the church, and they are serious convictions. The church is acknowledged as a specified Christian collaboration or group. Speaking further, the church is the children of God or Christian believers. As ministers of the Gospel, there is enjoyment in preaching and delivering sinners. Moreover, God expounds in Luke 15:7 that the Heavens become overjoyed when sinners become saints of God (KJV).

Additionally, deliverance can transpire while praising God. As we praise Him, our circumstances are revealed to be not as significant as we thought. This demonstration gives us the propensity to live free from downheartedness. There is power in praise! God inhabits the praises of His people; therefore, the performance of praising God is a catalyst, or substance, that stimulates a more spontaneous outcome.

Notwithstanding, wallowing in tribulations prolongs our deliverance. The power in praise ushers in the anointing of God, the anointing is stirred up within us, and outpoured upon us thus breaking and annihilating all bondages. For this purpose, we should praise God from sunrise to sunset. It is indispensable for Christians to comprehend how to have an enjoyable time in the Holy Ghost, even during times of affliction. As Paul motivated the Ephesians, likewise, Christians are to become overjoyed in the Holy Spirit through speaking scriptures, and singing Psalms, hymns, religious compositions that honor God, spiritual songs (joyful songs of praise), and outwardly and inwardly making lovely heartfelt melodies unto the Lord (Ephesians 5:19). Furthermore, always render thanksgiving to God, in Jesus' name, for everything. Thanksgiving is an exemplification of our love toward God, and Christians are to reverence God through honoring each other. If we continuously incorporate these demonstrations, we will remain filled with joy in the Holy Ghost.

Manifestation of the Holy Spirit: A Stronger Anointing

When I accepted the Lord as my personal Savior, the amount of joy that overwhelmed my soul was indescribable. My joy was so full, the thought of being acknowledged as a child of God whose sins were forgiven and forgotten, who was cleansed from all ungodliness, and who was filled with God's Spirit, is a moment that I will remember forever. I realized that the most consequential experience in life is to live an honorable lifestyle, and, therefore, please God always. Hearing the message of Jesus, and realizing it is better to marry than to burn caused me to become within appropriate alignment with the word of God, and seek God like never before. I accepted Him and sought Him wholeheartedly through consecrating, meditating, fasting, and praying, which became fundamental obligations. The submergence of His anointing percolated throughout me, the effervescence of the life of God both indwelt and stimulated myself, the benevolence of God's kindness and mercifulness was shown me, and my life was transformed forevermore.

As I traveled through my Christian journey, I desired the Holy Ghost with the evidence of speaking in tongues. God predetermines this gift. However, 1 Corinthians 12:10-11 unveils the manifestation of the gifts of the Spirit, one of which is the gift of different kinds of tongues (KJV). I prayed in faith that I would have my Pentecostal experience. I wanted to become sumptuously lavished in the Glory of God. Throughout times of prayer, worship, and consecration, God blessed me with the gift to speak with different tongues for several minutes up to four hours at a time.

One day, glory to God, my husband and I determined to relocate from Florida to Georgia. Previous to our departure, I began to pray, and unexpectedly, an unfathomable volume of God's anointing overshadowed me and overflowed my very being. The Spirit of God took control of my mouth, and I began speaking in tongues through the utterance of the Holy Ghost, praising and praying in miscellaneous languages until we arrived in Georgia. I was so pumped and primed in God. My communication with Him outstretched nine hours.

Correspondingly, throughout my Christian journey, singing in heavenly languages became desirous. Once again, God accommodated me. I have experienced the fullness of joy in the Holy Spirit, and I am so grateful to God for granting me the opportunity to experience such an enormous manifestation. This was unquestionably phenomenal. God is an astoundingly wondrous God. To be solidified in Him, and experiencing strength in the Holy Ghost, should be every Christians' anticipation. Nonetheless, the Gift of speaking with unknown tongues provisions Saints of God with superabundant joy and power, especially when Satan throws a curve ball into your life with intentions of exterminating your joy. Remember, the Lord's joy is your strength. It is given to you, not the Devil; therefore, practice it when he interferes with your existence.

For illustration, I have family members who are critical toward me for being overweight, and by them, I am referenced as "big Blondie" and "fat a••." This is tremendously painful. Throughout my life, I struggled with my weight. I tried to incorporate healthier meal plans, but it was problematical maintaining an innovative menu board. I literally had a relative tap me on my behind, as she pushed it in, telling me how hard it is, and how every time she sees me, I look larger and larger. I never comprehend how individuals have the audacity to believe it is their responsibility to investigate the tenderness or hardness of an individual's behind. This is not acceptable, and it is downright offensive. This disparaging commentary was extremely discouraging. I remember being brought to tears on numerous occasions. All the same, we have to love without dissimilation. As a result, I started meditating on God and His goodness. I casted my concerns and cares upon the Lord, remained prayerful, continued to love myself, and circumvented disheartening and demoralizing environments. Subsequently, I triumphed over others' opinions. In spite of everything, we must love unconditionally.

Living above my circumstances through the power of praise is what kept me joyful. However, these relatives, after having children, averaged between 150 to 160 pounds. Nowadays, they are over 300 pounds with multiplicities of incurable infections. I am not laughing at their consequences; nevertheless, these individuals cursed their personal physiques speaking deleteriously concerning others' and mine. It is more intelligent to utilize our mouths for uplifting the name of Jesus, praying for our adversaries, and motivating individuals.

Throughout the years, singing in Heavenly languages, without a doubt, provided empowerment during life's difficulties. To experience multidimensional elevations within the supernatural realm introduced me to a superabundance of joy I never knew.

Remember: Joy is equivalent to strength;
To become joyful is to become powerful
~ Blondie Williams ~

The Spirit of Forgiveness
CHAPTER 5

*W*hat does it means to have the spirit of forgiveness? The spirit of forgiveness is a God-given ability that provision people with the capability of providing remission or forgiveness for wrongdoings against them. Particularly, Christians are required to practice forgiveness at all times. If anyone proclaims to be a born-again child of God and does not demonstrate this gift, it is categorically sinful. Fundamentally, the Bible's explication of forgiveness has two dimensions; firstly, God's forgiveness towards our transgressions, and secondly, our forgiveness toward others' trespasses. This illustration of love is important and where we spend eternity is dependent upon us both comprehending and appropriating this biblical conceptualization.

In actuality, this redemption frees oneself as well as bringing freedom to the perpetrator. Theoretically speaking, forgiveness is activated by love. God showed His love toward mankind by sending His Son, Jesus, to give His life to save ours through the acceptance of Jesus, thus delivering us from iniquity. Ephesians 1:7 states our redemption came through Jesus' blood and our remission of sins were provided according to the riches of God's grace. We must never forget the love of God shown us. Therefore, we should forgive individuals who trespass against us. In Matthew 18:21, Peter asked Jesus, "How frequently should I forgive individuals that trespass against me? Seven times? Jesus responded, 'Until seventy times seven'" (KJV).

Forgiveness exemplifies the grace of God. Because Christians are new creations in Christ Jesus, we must always be forgivers. Consequently, in every circumstance, God's grace is sufficient for me. In reference to my disrespectful relatives criticizing me, I forgave those kinfolks on unquantifiable occasions. Nevertheless, God's grace prevailed every time. I came to the conclusion that entering particular environments is not advantageous. However, we must live in peaceful environments. Mark 11:25 reminds me when praying, if I remember I am angry with an individual, I must forgive that person so my Father God will forgive my wrongdoings. It is profitable to become spiritually navigated by God and Christians should become cognizant in acknowledging how to circumvent wicked or evil appearances. Howbeit, wickedness is always of the Devil. Christians should never become emotionally overtaken in guilt sidestepping negative individuals and destructive surroundings, for this is in our best interest. We are still soldiers in God's spiritual military and we are scripturally prepared in warfare. Therefore, our shield of faith utterly exterminates Satan's darts of wickedness, especially in the illustration concerning my family. Unfortunately, I cannot control how individuals treat me; fortunately, I can control how I treat them. My determination is to please God through demonstrating the spirit of forgiveness and love through heartfelt smiles and greetings. Characteristically, it is consequential to me that continuity in God's love and grace are projected.

"Forgiveness is two-dimensional: God's
forgiveness toward Christians and Christians'
forgiveness toward others
~ Blondie Williams ~

Conquering the Workings of Satan
CHAPTER 6

There are three adversarial enemies: a worldly mind, the human flesh, and demonic spirits. These adversaries are continuously attempting to bring devastation against a Christian's privileges and existence in accordance with a spiritually constructive standard of living. Three systematical developments to subjugating these three adversaries encompass overpowering worldly lusts through the power of God's love, dominating human flesh through the possession of the Holy Ghost, and vanquishing Satan through the powerful name of Jesus. The Bible tells saints in 1 John 3:8 that individuals who exhibit unprincipled functionalities are children of the Devil; for this reason, the manifestation of the Son of God appeared so He would demolish the devil's workings (KJV). Let us understand the differentiations between worldly desires, human flesh, and Satan.

Worldly Desires:

A worldly consciousness is characterized as developing affection for and devotion toward worldly fascinations or interests. Worldly fascinations might integrate modeling nude in magazines, starring in pornographic movies, and married couples attending sex parties, engaging in open marriages, and practicing homosexuality, for illustration. These interests should not be implemented, especially by children of God. Our consciousness should never be managed by the Devil or his worldly lusts, which is a strong longing or pining to have something. An additional example, consider a woman who desires to have another woman's husband, or a man who desires to have another man's wife. With that being said, so many Christians have allowed the adversary to manipulate their cognizance to participate in these prototypical fascinations. It is time to take our minds from the Devil, and give them back to God. Worldly or carnal psychological reasoning or mindsets generate spiritual death, causing Saints to become contradictory toward God thus becoming His enemies. To become rooted and grounded in the characterizations of Christ causes Christians to become planted, steadfastly or unfalteringly within Him, and enjoying an incorruptible life full of spiritual harvest.

Never transmogrify yourselves to the configuration of worldly persons, but rather, epitomize Godly propensities of thinking. Christians are supposed to demonstrate spiritual courageousness to maintain a theologically persuaded consciousness thus circumnavigating psychological adaptations and fascinations that strengthen their spiritual minds and gratify their souls. In general, this means Christians' feelings, viewing platforms, dispositions, and predominating attitudes must demonstrate strong interests concerning ecclesiastical requirements, if they, as Christians, desire to defeat the adversary of worldly consciousness through continuously mediating upon God and accomplishing His will.

Remember: To which spirit you surrender
your mind and body, is the spirit that you will
become possessed by ~ Blondie Williams ~

Human Flesh:

The composition of humankind is distinguished as a psychological structure that encompasses an outer physical substance (flesh), and is provisioned as a covering or house for the human inner spirit. The human flesh is an adversarial enemy because it can deteriorate a Christian characteristically and dissipate his or her anointing in the Holy Ghost. Remain cognizant of the fact that sin stimulates a disconnection between God and His children. First Corinthians 6:19-20 of The New Open Bible ascertains that our bodies belong to God, for they are temples of the Holy Spirit, which is endowed upon us and given to us for His utilization (TNOB - KJV).

The Holy Ghost leads and guides us throughout all our concerns and affairs in life. Therefore, this endowment guarantees that if we unresistingly follow its unction, we will become victorious over fleshly sensations and tendencies, which is substantial for effective Christian discipleship. We should never have this destructive enemy (the human flesh), with its deprivations, become influential within any component of our lives. Although, some individuals will experience such struggles more than others, do not allow these temptations to become fascinations. Take out the big guns, so to speak, within your arsenal, and fight conscientiously to keep your flesh under spiritual management through the power of the Holy Spirit. "For greater is He that is within you than He that is within the world" (1 John 4:4 TNOB - KJV).

Do not contaminate your spirit, for Heaven is at stake!

Demonic Spirits:

Demonic spirits is the third antagonist. The tempter, Satan, endeavors to sabotage Christians' effectiveness by unleashing demonic spirits to harass our minds and lives. The Devil is an enemy to both God and Christians. He is a disobedient fallen angel who was prohibited from Heaven. This adversary is often acknowledged as Beelzebub or Lucifer. The Bible tells us in 1 Peter 5:8 to demonstrate self-control and to always be watchful because the Devil journeys back and forth, roaring as a lion, and searching for individuals to demolish (TNOB - KJV). Remaining steadfast and unmovable in the faith of God provides Saints with resistance towards the Devil. By resisting him, he will ultimately depart from us. Maintaining freedom from these three adversarial antagonisms—worldly thinking, the human flesh, and the Devil—is mandatory if we are to live productively as Christian disciples.

Christian Discipleship
CHAPTER 7

What is Christian discipleship? Christian discipleship is definitive of individuals that have accepted indoctrination as an ecclesiastical follower of Jesus. These Disciples of Christ are committed and dedicated to spreading apostles' doctrines throughout the world and believe the Holy Bible is the exclusive publication to be employed in Christian religion to particularize apostolic faith, evangelic procedurals, regulatory bible principles, Christian attitudes, Christian performances, and standards of judgments. Correspondingly, administration of and participation within a baptismal ceremony, and membership within a congregational apostolicity, additionally characterize Christian discipleship. What is more, authentic discipleships are picturesquely endowed as Disciples of Christ who have sanctified themselves from the world.

Our focalization should always be in alignment with biblical doctrines through not only being hearers of theologies regarding Jesus but also doers of those theological standardizations (James 1:22). Furthermore, Christians are to keep God at the head of their lives, first in everything by making sure to ask Him for direction. It is transparently expounded in Philippians 3:8-9 that all things are worth nothing compared to the invaluableness of knowing Christ Jesus our Lord. Because of Him, though I have suffered loss of everything, those things became worthless next to winning through knowing and establishing a relationship with Christ. Overall, it is through giving up immoral principles of living that causes us to belong to Him and become His Disciples (KJV).

In Matthew 28:18-20, Jesus told His disciples that He was given all power in Heaven and in Earth. Therefore, through the power of His spirit, Disciples of Christ must go forth converting individuals and making disciples out of them, baptizing them in the name of the Father, in the name of the Son, and in the name of the Holy Ghost. Correspondingly, Disciples should also teach new converts to always be obedient toward everything Jesus instructed and commanded, and to always remember that Jesus is forever with them, even unto the end of the world (KJV). I hearten you to maintain strong fellowship with your fellow brethren in the Lord, for worshipping God ecclesiastically and congregationally strengthen our Christian relationships, enabling us to continue itinerating up the King's highway and remaining faithful to His agenda.

Christian Fellowship

Christian Fellowship is comprehended as a friendly inter-relation between individuals who share common interests and mutual attitudes concerning their life experiences. Christian experiences are shared through church memberships or spiritual partnerships. Fellowship involves socialization, which might incorporate a collaborative group of believers congregating within fellowship halls, annex centers, places of worship, gospel meetings, as well as engaging in wholesome spiritual discussions during face to face conversations or telecommunications. Brothers and sisters, deacons and deaconesses, or ministers and clergypersons enjoying the presence of God through each other within Holy Communion services, Bible studies, Christian concerts, church picnics, spiritual fitness walks, or whether visiting members' homes for lunch are supplementary demonstrations of Christian fellowship.

Subsequent Christians' adoption into the family of God, we have effective fellowship with Him and our brothers and sisters in Christ. It is important that we understand the significance of the Christian family dynamic. Our Father, God, delights in His children walking in love, in unity, and in fellowship through His Spirit. Ephesians 1:5 reminds us that God "predestined us to be adopted as his sons through Jesus Christ, in accordance with his pleasure and will" (KJV). Thank God for being an adopted child of God! When seeking fellowship, always choose believers like yourselves. Amos 3:3 asks, "Can two walk together except they be in agreement?" (KJV). No, because two can only walk in agreement if they are children of God, for we are interconnected through His love and His Spirit, which are one. In essence, to walk in Christian fellowship is equivalent to walking in Christian love. Harmonious and joyous spirits are stimulated from the love and laughter that customarily transcend from family member to family member.

Second Corinthians 6:14-18 KJV communicates:

Be not unequally yoked together with unbelievers for what fellowship hath righteousness with unrighteousness? And what communion hath light with darkness? And what concord hath Christ with Be-li-al? Or what part hath he that believeth with an infidel? And what agreement hath the temple of God with idols? For ye are the temple of the living God; as God hath said, I will dwell in them; and walk in them; and I will be their God, and they shall be my people. Wherefore come out from among them, and be ye separate, saith the Lord, and touch not the unclean thing; and I will receive you. And will be a Father unto you, and ye shall be my sons and daughters, saith the Lord Almighty.

Do not become paired together with nonbelievers.
Righteousness and wickedness have nothing in common,
for you share common interests with your spiritual family
memberships through Christian fellowship
~ Blondie Williams ~

Christian Fellowship

Oh, what sweet communion

In God's only Son;

Loving Christian fellowship-

Hearts united as one;

Joined together in Christ,

Free from the state of sin,

Adoring the King of kings-

Our very closest Friend.

One common purpose,

And one single goal-

To glorify our Saviour

Till heavens gates unfold.

"...if we walk in the light, as he is in the light, we have fellowship one with another, and the blood of Jesus Christ his Son cleanseth us from all sin" (I John 1:7 KJV).

By Connie Campbell Bratcher

Christian Stewardship

What is Christian stewardship? Christian stewardship is a biblical principle that helps Christians understand how to appropriately manage themselves, God's gifts, and everything God entrusts them with. Stewardship is beneficial in children of God, making qualitative and quantitative determinations throughout their Christian journeys which reverence God and transform the world. God has ownership of the universe and everything within it (Whelchel, 2017). Psalm 24:1 elucidates, "The earth is the Lord's and the fullness thereof; the world, and they that dwell there" (KJV).

Theologically speaking, exemplifications of Christian stewardship illustrate Christians' management of how their time is used publicly, privately, and spiritually; how their ecclesiastical talents or gifts are utilized; how their material possessions are expended; and how their monetary blessings are distributed among ministerial services. It is paramount to remember that superlative stewardship management interconnects governance over both household family interactions and household family expenditures. What is more, Christian stewardship is demonstrative of believers being lovers of God, and educating and training their children to love and honor Him through accepting Jesus, living Christian lifestyles, and educating other Disciples about the principles of stewardship. Stewards correspondingly make provisions for their families and secure their families' futures. This is done through fathers working to the sweat of their brows and making knowledgeable financial investments, for laziness is not godliness (Whelchel, 2017).

In the parable of the talents described within Matthew 25:14-30, God explained to Christian stewards about the inducements involved with advantageously capitalizing their investments. This parable associates the kingdom of heaven to a man taking an excursion into a different countryside, calling forth his servants and distributing his possessions to them before disembarking. He disbursed five talents to one steward, two talents to another steward, and one talent to the remaining servant. He conscientiously apportioned to every servant according to his proportional capability. Chronologically, the servant who was given five talents doubled his investment opportunity by five talents, and the servant who was provided two talents capitalized his investment by two talents, doubling his financial investment, and the steward who received one talent did not attempt to compound his investment; instead, he dug a hole, and afterward hid his master's finances into the earth. This particular servant, however, is illustrative of a slothful or unproductive servant. When their master returned from his journey, he collaborated with the servants to differentiate what were the consequences of their financial investments. The unproductive servant's master told him that he should have placed his investment with investment bankers or exchangers so that accumulate a profitable return. After which, the master retrieved the four talents from the servant who doubled his master's two talents and distributed them to the servant that doubled his master's five talents. The unprofitable servant was thrown into outer darkness. In contrasting view, the two servants who diligently sought to make intelligent investments through doubling their talents were told "well done." The master further proclaimed that they were good and faithful servants, and acknowledged that they were faithful concerning a few things, and, therefore, he was going to make them sovereign over many things. Afterwards, the productive stewards were ushered into the joy of the Lord (KJV).

Christian stewardship is qualitatively
supervising our God-given resources: our
families, finances, and ecclesiastical and
evangelical ministrations.

Abusing God's Patience
CHAPTER 8

This chapter is segmented into powerful inspirations encompassing my personal experiences to motivate Christians experiencing hardships to never abuse God's patience through doubting. Desperate times call for desperate measures; therefore, remain prayerful and watchful with thanksgiving. The Bible teaches us to trust and never doubt. It is important to remember submitting to God's Word is a priority, and faith pleases Him. So hold on, soldier, and fight the good fight of faith. Your patience will cause you to triumph! On that note, what are you going to do, walk in faith or drown in disbelief?

Have you, as Saints of God, ever disregarded the feeling of conviction within your spirit? You tried overlooking the fact that you failed to perform in a capacity that pleased God.

We acknowledge that sin is unacceptable behavior before God and before true children of God. Some Christians travel throughout life committing sinful performances, deceived by the Devil into believing that it is fine to sin as long as you repent following the sinful deed. This is a misconception of how Saints of God should perform throughout their lives. Get to know God for yourselves. People will tell you anything for their own personal reasons; besides, there are no excuses when it comes to spiritual disobedience. Matthew 10:16 outlines the fact that as Christians, God sends us out as sheep amongst wolves, and encourages us to be wise as serpents, yet humble as doves (KJV). Therefore, we are to analyze individual conversations and spiritual leadership instructions through discernment or the gift of discerning spirits to establish whether or not individuals are telling or teaching us the truth, regardless of what their title or position is.

In Matthew 7:15, God reminds us to beware of false prophets, who come to you camouflaged in sheep's clothing, but inwardly they are malicious and ferocious wolves (KJV). The same applies to any fictitious teacher or leader. Contradictory to what anyone feels, these individuals exist. Awkwardly enough, I personally, had a "bishop" attempt to disadvantageously influence me to have sex with an old flame from my sinful past. He learned that I do not have STDs, HIV, or AIDS, and that the old flame did. In view of that, this bishop's wife informed me that the pair of them has incurable STDs and full-blown AIDS. What is more, this so-called "bishop" said to me, "I do not understand why you are so concerned with contracting such diseases." He further explicated that most individuals have an incurable disease and/or HIV, and stated we all—referencing his mutual acquaintances—have AIDS, so what is the difference if you acquired it? I thought this was the most disrespectful suggestion any human being has ever made to me, especially for a "bishop". I was unquestionably flabbergasted. Not that I considered it, but to engage in such activity would call for me to, firstly, disregard God's Holy written Word; secondly, participate in premarital sex; and thirdly, acquire communicable diseases willfully and deliberately (although, Jesus bore our sins and diseases in His body so that we could live spiritually and physiologically healthy lives). Regardless, according to this bishop, I was supposed to have contradicted the Word of Truth to satisfy him?

To deliberately choose to live with such physiological deteriorations to make this so-called bishop live more comfortably within himself is unequivocally ridiculous. Some sexually transmitted sicknesses cause visual complications and eventually blindness. And, to be asked to purposefully accept a spirit of infirmity is appalling. Who does that? Me, commit disobedience to God through intentionally formicating against my body? I think not. Wretchedness or misery loves company, for sure.

I am a redeemed child of God, and I am astronomically proud of it. I stood solidified in God, refused to get in touch with that old flame, and maintained dignity, decency, and self-respect in the process. I truly love this entitlement for my book: "Solidified in God—the Devil is defeated. I comprehend that men and women of the cloth, and supplementary Christians, are supposed to travel throughout the world teaching and preaching against sin, and persuading sinners to accept Jesus as Lord and Savior. We, as soldiers in God's army, should do specifically that: teach against sin. Be watchful of these types of individuals. Perchance you encountered them, and became brainwashed by the "do it and pray" lifestyle, which means sinning as you will, but not forgetting to pray, and two breaths previous to death, repent for your sins so you will be received into heaven.

I assure you this teaching and such a lifestyle is displeasing before God. With the "do it and pray" mentality, when will these individuals ever grow spiritually? Where are their works? They will become complacent with wickedness and never live their lifecycles in capacities that please God. In consequence, they will lose against Satan. Satan is a defeated foe, neither God nor you are. This lifestyle is for losers; if Christians are to become winners, they must put aside the weight and sin of the world so they are capable of uncomplainingly or patiently running the race that God has set before them. It is unambiguously impossible for Christians to commit wrongdoings and the Holy Spirit not convicts their hearts.

When you feel such conviction, examine yourself and comprehend your immoral performances, then acknowledge them to God in prayer. It is not beneficial to rationalize your derogatory behavior, thinking that God is unmindful concerning you, therefore, He missed it. I serve you notice that it is impossible to get over on God; He misses nothing. Proverbs 15:3 pronounces "The eyes of the Lord are in every place, beholding the evil and the good" (KJV).

Psalm 50:21 embolden us to remember that the quietness of Heaven is no indication that God supports mischief. He cares if we sin, and all sinners will be punished (TLB). Be cognizant of the inevitability that remaining in sin is abusive to the patience of God. It should never become a conception in our minds that momentary gratification is worthwhile and not the spirit of obedience just because God does not discipline us instantaneously. The weight of conviction is essentially an invitation to refrain from transgressions and demonstrate righteousness and holiness.

A devout passion in God is what Christians must return. This enables us to not abuse God's patience through trusting that He is observant concerning our everyday performances; let us not take advantage of His kindness. Although He loves us and understands our struggles, never treat Him as though He is ignorant because He is not chastising us spontaneously. In due season, He will reward every one of us according to our works; if our reflections were sinful, we will receive punishment. So, become transformed within your hearts, minds, and spirits, and serve your kind and forgiving Father single-mindedly and wholeheartedly.

Patience Is Compensated

The Holy Scriptures share countless stories of individuals who trusted and waited weeks, months, years, or even decades prior to the manifestation of God's promises. What might the modern-day Disciples learn about the patience of God from the monarch David? Firstly, waiting patiently on God has everlasting benefits. David, Israel's most unforgettable monarch was the sovereign beneficiary to Israel's throne, and he exhausted immeasurable years in circumvention of King Saul's wrath. Although David had two different opportunities to take out vengeance against Saul he withstood the temptation to utterly destroy Saul, instead choosing to spare his life. David determined to abide by God's appointed schedule for his crowning ceremony alternative to disgracing his Father by assassinating King Saul. Moreover, David's song of praise divulged his cherished consciousness of God's work within his life. King David both accomplished his objective through patience and observance of his Father's omniscience. God always knows what is best for His children. David, in turn, left an extraordinarily powerful testimonial of God's divine faithfulness for His children to study and meditate upon. David was definitely dedicated to waiting upon the Lord; accordingly, he became approved and blessed of his Father. Never underestimate the eternal reward provided us through living within God's divine favor. The favor of God is not a specialized state of being earmarked for faith giants such as the monarch King David. Everyone who faithfully and obediently withstands until Jehovah (the God who provides) moves on his or her behalf abides within His favor. Consequently, David was not showered with blessings because he was a special king. David was momentously honored throughout the population because he honored God significantly above everything. Because David trusted in Jehovah's faithfulness, he went through hardships with patience. As God's children, through waiting patiently upon the Lord, we can anticipate being blessed and favored through God's love (In Touch Ministries, 2016).

Desperate Times Call for Desperate Measures

As King David was a great example of a faith giant, the Apostle Paul is another illustration. Paul comprehended how to effectively handle hard-hitting and uncompromising experiences. When Paul was incarcerated, he kept his eyes upon his Savior and unwaveringly trusted Him. For that reason, although he was chained in the penitentiary, Paul celebrated the work of the Lord in his life. Truthfully, Paul constructed an epistle from the penitentiary to the Philippians jam-packed with jubilation. Concentrating upon the Savior is neither a natural nor a simplistic response. Our predisposition as Christians is to not dwell upon our circumstances. I know, at times, some Christians become overwhelmed by pondering over their adversities. They begin searching for solutions on their own accords, focalizing upon the discomfort associated with enduring harsh conditions, and becoming impatient while waiting upon God. Consequently, these Christians feel as though they are defeated. It is important to acknowledge that fearfulness cannot reside for elongated periods of time within the heart of individuals that trust in the Lord. Therefore, it is necessitous that Christians continuously think of the goodness of Jesus, for doing so motivates Christians. Remember, Jehovah Jirah is the God who provides. He is a deliverer (2 Corinthians 1:10). He is a healer (Matthew 4:23). He is a navigator (Proverbs 3:6). He provides us with everything we need, for He promised. Therefore, believers who hold fast to God's divine promises discover that He removes negative feelings and emotions. Our Father substitutes negative emotions with positive feelings of hope, assurance, and contentment. Biblical principles or the promises of God do not fluctuate, so regardless of how penetrating or excruciating the circumstances, emphasis should be placed upon God, not your circumstances. The Holy Spirit of God is a comforter, and He will comfort your spirit and your heart as He brings you through your hardships. A greater strength comes from responding as Paul did when he was under confinement, which was to rejoice in the Lord always (In Touch Ministries, 2016).

Submission

It is important for Saints to become submissive to God, yield to a superior dynamism, or submit to the spirit or authority of another. The dynamism of God demands Christians to become in absolute submission to His authority. His Word is His authority; therefore, Christian submission to the righteousness of God is a must. Throughout our lives, it is mandatory that we follow the Holy Spirit in everything. Submission establishes Christians as well-trained children of God who understand how to control their environments. Ephesians 5:21 states, "submit you one to another in the fear of God" (KJV). 1 Peter 5:5 states:

Likewise, ye younger people, submit yourselves unto elder individuals. Everyone must become subject to each other and become clothed in humility.

God withstands or resists the proud, and extends grace to the humble. It is up to individuals how they perform throughout their home environments (KJV).

It is significant that the spirit of humbleness overshadows Christians' lives. Submission must be demonstrated within marriages. Colossians 3:18 encourages the submission of wives unto their own husbands, for this is acceptable before the Lord. Submission must be demonstrated towards your ecclesiastical leaderships through recognizing their authority over you, for they are keeping watch over your souls and continually guarding your spiritual welfare as, standing as stewards who will give an account for you (Hebrews 13:17 AMP). Therefore, allow them to perform this within the spirit of joy, and not grief: for that is unprofitable for you (Hebrews 13:17 KJV).

In other words, The Message states that Christian submission means to be responsive to your pastoral leaderships. Listen to their counsel, knowing they function under strict supervision of the spirit of God. Contribute to the joy of their leadership, not its drudgery. Why would you want to make things harder for them? (Hebrews 13:17 MSG). In addition, the submission of parents is influential toward the submission of their children. Salvation resolves iniquity. To become born again through faith in God is a demonstration of your submission to Him, to the deity and power of His authority, which is His Word, and submission to Jesus as God's Son which means your salvation.

Submission is, correspondingly, the soul of discipleship. Jesus called Christians to both believe and follow Him. As previously stated, a disciple is an apprentice and follower who submitted himself or herself to his or her teacher for instruction. Fundamentally, submission has protuberant themes throughout the Christian life. For illustration, submission is comprehended as limited concerning nonspiritual submission, and unlimited regarding biblical submission; nonspiritual submission is unavoidable, yet executed externally, and biblical submission is voluntary, whereas, it is stimulated from the heart. Respectively, nonreligious submission is motivated through self-interest, and religious submission is encouraged through conviction, expectation, and adoration, resulting in unselfishness. Worldly submission is prearranged for authoritative individuals who anticipate or demand that people conduct themselves within capacities that benefit them, and holy submission is provided to individuals who surrendered their worldly privileges to bless the body of Christ. Nonspiritual submission is predominantly contingent upon authority, and scriptural submission is contingent upon priority, which is indicative of placing other's interests before yours. Additionally, non-scriptural submission endeavors to minimalize dependency upon other individuals, and maximize a person's individualistic independence. In conclusion, biblical submission accentuates our interdependence upon each other, for God works through His children to bless the world (Deffinbaugh, 2017).

Remember to submit to one another out of reverence for Christ.

Will You Walk in Faith or Sink in Doubt?
CHAPTER 9

$\mathcal{F}$aith is a powerful tool; through it, there is nothing on this planet that we cannot handle. God always has His hands extended to help us maintain our balance if we stumble. If our faith is challenged, and we find it difficult to remain afloat, remember God is only an arm's length away. If we walk in faith, we will not sink in doubt. As Peter walked on water, he became doubtful and frightful, and only then did he began to sink. Jesus straightaway stretched out his hand and laid hold of Peter, and asked him was he of little faith, and why did he become doubtful (Matthew 14:31 KJV).

Atmospherically speaking, the Bible describes the Galilean environment as dark and boisterously windy, and the windstorm caused the Sea of Galilee to experience ferocious waves that aggressively tossed the ship Jesus and His disciples occupied. Although, several of the disciples were seasoned fisherman as was Peter, still, they became frightened. When Jesus' disciples thought the uncontrolled blustery winds and waves would force them underneath the water, Jesus walked on the water toward them as they cried out nervously. Therefore, Jesus instantaneously spoke to them, comforting their spirits, saying, "Be of good cheer; it is I. be not afraid" (Matthew 14:24-27 KJV).

Just as Peter took his eyes off the Lord, paying more attention to what was going on around him, so do many Christians. Our eyes should be fixated upon the Lord the instant we start to concentrate upon the inclement weather that, at times, rages within our lives unless we began to sink. As Saints of God, when we feel ourselves slipping downward, we must, through faith, believe that God will stretch out His hand and lift us to safety regardless of our circumstance. I encourage you all to keep your eyes on God; He is a caring Father who has the omnipotence to rescue us from troublesome times. Remember that God is bigger than our predicaments (In Touch Ministries, 2016).

So, what will you do? Walk in faith or sink in doubt?

Faith Above Fear

Nowadays, with everything going on around us, there are numerous reasons to become fearful. This world appears to be within a catastrophic predicament for one reason or another. The employment marketplace is disappointing, natural disasters are wreaking devastation, and news media headlines concerning criminality are dominating propagations (widespread news broadcastings). As children of God, we thoroughly understand that fear is an enemy of God's, and that fear should not be permitted within any place throughout our lives. Nonetheless, we might question ourselves—how is it possible to ignore what is taking place around us? Fundamentally, we have one of two alternatives: to walk in faith or to walk in fear. It is without question impossible to believe and doubt God simultaneously. Fractional obedience is disobedience.

Therefore, I ask, in which direction is your spiritual navigation directing your travel? Faith Street or Fear Avenue? Individuals who study the Holy Bible and believe God, at times, decide to travel down Fear Avenue. Such people observe others experiencing hardships and begin wondering to themselves if such adversities could happen to them. For illustration, if an associate was terminated from his position, a person who walks in fear would begin questioning if he would be released from his occupation as well. As another example, if a fearful person's girlfriend passed away following an automobile collision, he might begin thinking he could experience the same fate.

Do not position your circumstances above your relationship with your Father. However, if Satan can manipulate you psychologically to think in such capacity, he has categorically won the battle within your mind. I encourage your spirits to concentrate on God, which is His Word. Never believe the Devil, for he is the father of deception and lies. Moreover, he is your Father's enemy, and therefore, he should be yours.

I embolden you, my brothers and sisters, whenever you become vigilant to God, alternate to the Devil, you become a winner. Remember, fear is an enemy of believers. Our affectionate and compassionate Father comprehends our sufferings, reservations, doubts, and disappointments. We must acknowledge that His Holy Spirit is an encouraging Spirit, which speaks to our hearts and minds to assist us in understanding that He is sufficient for our every need. To receive these biblical truths throughout your lives will unquestionably exterminate the spirit of worry from you so God can elevate you above your heartaches and tribulations and outpour His blessings throughout your lives. Keep the faith! Go forth, children of God! Forever travel down Faith Street, and in doing so, experience an amazing Christian journey (In Touch Ministries, 2016).

The Victorious Soldier

God is a wonderful Father who has a predetermined schedule or plan for the lives of His children. However, the Devil places stumbling blocks within our route from earth to eternal Heaven. There are numerous obstructions this archfiend releases against God's beloved children. These might involve injurious supervisors, adulterous husbands or wives, rebellious children, jealous co-workers, incongruous family memberships, or budgetary inconsistencies. Beelzebub's main objective is to block Christians from functioning at their best.

One thing I am appreciative of is that the Devil can never touch Christians' lives without God's approval. Always remember whatever Satan throws within your passageway will never destroy anything concerning your life because he is a defeated foe. God does not give His children blessings for Satan to bulldoze believers and steal their blessings. Your blessings are yours!

Joshua's army was unmatched in comparison to Jericho's armed forces. The great wall that protected the city of Jericho was an impossible barricade to maneuver beyond. Even so, God promised the Israelites a proportionate division of land, and Joshua believed God. He never thought the blessing would be denied him. Joshua acknowledged God's anointing and he stood unswayable in God's instructions, for Joshua knew God had worked everything out in favor of His children. God was working, thus preparing the city of Jericho for total destruction through placing the spirit of fear inside kings throughout the country. God's instructions involved a strategically implemented approach—operation battalion, for instance. Joshua demonstrated nothing less than obedience to God; as a consequence, God's children triumphed. The process of waiting can be difficult. At times, we begin to contemplate if our Father will come to our rescue. Then, His Holy Spirit comforts and encourages us to continue to wait upon God, for with Him, failure is never an option.

Thank God for being our comforter, because without Him, we will utterly fail through giving up. Throwing in the towel is simplistic if you do not trust your Father. God has already prepared a way for us as He did for Joshua. Regardless of how God determines to handle our problems, His solutions are always most beneficial to His children. Therefore, in the midst of any stumbling block, we must not allow Satan the advantage. We must continue to humbly pray and trust God because the Devil is the defeated one, not God's children (In Touch Ministries, 2016).

Remember, many things might
entangle our feet, but none of
them shall hold us fast.

The Phenomenal Existence of God
CHAPTER 10

*G*od is omniscient. Omniscience is demarcated as God's capability of knowing everything. He is a sovereign God and creator of all visible and invisible things. His omniscience is not constrained to a particularized person within the spiritual Godhead. The Godhead incorporates the Trinitarian doctrine, which describes the most Holy Trinity as a religious devout family that is acknowledged, accepted, and honored as the Father, the Son, and the Holy Ghost comprehensively omniscient in nature.

As Christians, it is indispensable for us to become informed through God's spirit, for this is consequential throughout our human existence and throughout our human relationships.

Educational intelligence is important, for it is essential in the acquisition of information *vis-à-vis* the development of personal aptitudes pedagogically, occupationally, physiologically, and domestically. In addition, personal standards, moralities, philosophies, behaviors, attitudes, and everyday functionalities are understood through the educational process. Nevertheless, God's understanding is omniscient. Therefore, Christians are to become the epitome of our Father; we must beseech God for His wisdom and understanding in everything. It is more qualitative to become well-balanced intellectually both academically and spiritually.

To further comprehend our Father's omniscience, the terminology is categorized into two interconnected morphologies. *Omni*, which is descriptive of altogether or all and science, and is symptomatic of knowledge or being unboundedly intellectual. Theologically speaking, there are three *omnis* that represent the essence of God: omniscience, all knowing; omnipotence, all-powerful; and omnipresence, all places at the same time (Temple, n.d.).

Confirmation of God's Omniscience

"For if our heart condemn us, God is greater than our heart, and knoweth all things" (1 John 3:20 KJV).

> When we become convicted, God comforts us in knowing that He knows our heart; therefore, He will assist us in controlling our emotions, and praying to Him to get acquitted from our convictions.

"Before I formed thee in the belly I knew thee; and before thou camest forth out of the womb I sanctified thee, and ordained thee a prophet unto the nations" (Jeremiah 1:5 KJV).

> Before I was birthed into this life, God formed and created me; then He consecrated and ordained me as Prophetess Blondie Williams. It is important to understand that God knew everyone before we were conceived within our mother's womb, and He knows our gifts, and our life's purpose.

"Great is our Lord, and mighty in power; His understanding is infinite" (Psalm 147:5 ASV).

Our Father epitomizes comprehensive astuteness, profuse strength, and inexpressible dominion. Everything we will ever require or desire throughout our lives, God, in His omniscience, is the anointing that causes it to materialize.

"But the very hairs of your head are all numbered" (Matthew 10:30 KJ21).

God knows everything about us, even the total aggregate of hair strands that are upon our heads. If we lose a few, He will never lose count.

"O Lord, thou hast searched me, and known me. Thou knowest my downsitting and mine uprising, thou understandest my thought afar off. Thou compassest my path and my lying down, and art acquainted with all my ways" (Psalm 139:1-3 KJ21).

Remember, God is an omniscient God who is knowledgeable of our daily activities, conversations, and interactions. I admonish you to always uphold biblical principles to guarantee the Devil does not embarrass you, but rather you please God through the spirit of obedience.

The Omnipotence of God demonstrates God's maximum power, maximum greatness, and total perfection. Traditional Western theism ascertains God is unambiguously omnipotent because of His greatness and perfectness. Omnipotence might appear to be confounding or paradoxical even to theologians; much contemplation has taken place to understand the omnipotence of God. Provided are implications implementing Holy Scriptures to provision assistance in thoroughly developing a comprehension of the nature of God (Zalta, Hoffman & Rosenkrantz, 2014).

Confirmation of God's Omnipotence

There are no impossibilities in God. Our God is astronomically great and extraordinarily powerful; His comprehension is fathomless.

> "Have you not known? Hast you not heard, the everlasting God, the Lord, the Creator of the ends of the earth, fainteth not, neither is weary? there is no searching of his understanding" (Isaiah 40:28 KJV).

"I know that thou canst do every thing, and that no thought can be witholden from thee" (Job 42:2 KJV).

These passages illuminate the actuality that God never becomes fatigued, and He is always performing His Word in the lives of His children. Additionally, He is all-knowledgeable, which means our Father knows our thoughts and performances previous to us forming them. His omnipotence is sovereign.

And what is the immeasurable greatness of his power toward us who believe, according to the working of his great might that he worked in Christ when he raised him from the dead and seated him at his right hand in the heavenly places, far above all rule and authority and power and dominion, and above every name that is named, not only in this age but also in the one to come. And he put all things under his feet and gave him as head over all things to the church. (Ephesians 1:19-22 ESV)

God's tremendous illustriousness was manifested to Saints of God the day He demonstrated His limitlessness through raising Jesus from the dead, positioning Him on His right hand

in the most majestic seat in Heaven, giving Him the most superlative name above all names, and placing Him over every ecclesiastical service concerning the church, thus acknowledging
Him throughout all spiritual endeavors.

> "And I heard as it were the voice of a great mul-
> titude, and as the voice of many waters, and as
> the voice of mighty thunderings, saying, Alleluia:
> for the Lord God omnipotent reigneth" (Revelation
> 19:6 KJV).

Hallelujah! The everlasting Father, the omnipotent God reigns
throughout all eternity!

The infinite omnipresence of God means He is everywhere
simultaneously. In Western theism, omnipresence is expounded
as God's ability to presence Himself everywhere at the same
time, thus speaking of the Supreme Being's unrestrained or
universal presence. Omnipresence is additionally described as
there being no place upon this earth in which God's understanding and power do not outspread. The Deity's presence
is unremitting throughout all of creation, although, it is not
revealed in the same capacity as it is toward individuals

everywhere. Sometimes, He is actively existent within particular states of affair, and yet may well not reveal His presence within different circumstances. However He is present for He promised to never leave us. Even if we do not feel His presence, be confident that He is present (Zalta, Hoffman & Rosenkrantz, 2014).

Moreover, His omnipresence is representative of being contemporaneous throughout all dimensions of time and space. God is everywhere and is always in the now. His omnipresence should uninterruptedly serve as a reminder to His children that even if we sin, there is no hiding place that our Father does not comprehend. Therefore, come out of hiding, wherever you are, and return to God remorseful and prayerful. He loves you! (Zalta, Hoffman & Rosenkrantz, 2014).

Confirmation of God's Omnipresence

"Can anyone hide himself in secret places that I shall not see him? The Lord said do not I fill heaven and earth?" (Jeremiah 23:24 KJV).

"The eyes of the Lord are in every place, beholding the evil and the good" (Proverbs 15:3 KJV).

"Everything was made by him; and without him was not anything made that was made" (John 1:3-5 KJV).

"And God is before all things, and by him all things consist" (Colossians 1:17 KJV).

"For his eyes are upon the ways of man, and he sees his entire goings" (Job 34:21 KJV).

"When you pass through the waters, I [will be] with thee; and through the rivers, they shall not overflow thee: when you walk through the fire, you shall not be burned; neither shall the flame kindle upon thee" (Isaiah 43:2 AMP).

> I am comprehensively convinced that nothing dead or anything alive, neither angels in heaven nor devils on earth, not even present things forthcoming things, not height nor depth, and neither any creature throughout all creation has the capability of separating children of God from His love, which was established in Christ Jesus (Romans 8:38-39).

Now that we understand the awesomeness of God and how His infallibility is acknowledged previously, contemporaneously, futuristically, and theologically, it is detrimental for the universe to fail to acknowledge Him. For the complete biosphere are God's, and the fullness thereof. This means all human beings, all territorial properties, all oceanic waters, all sea creatures, all land animals, and everything that inhabits this planet belongs to God.

As I mentioned previously, I read and studied God's unfailing Word from Genesis to Revelation at sixteen years of age, and, throughout my journey, He penetrated me with His knowledge. He is unquestionably omniscient. By the time I completed my journey, His infallible Word had infiltrated my very heart, spirit, and soul; I have never felt so full spiritually. This accomplishment caused me to fall in love with God through His anointing. God's anointing is representative of aromatic oil outpoured upon the crown of an individual's head unto the sole of his or her feet. Supernaturally, as I studied the Holy Bible, my experience was breathtaking; I felt rehabilitated, transformed, and intellectualized beyond words. The anointing of God possessed my entire body, both inside and outside. My spirit smiled interminably as I thoughtfully listened to the voice of my Father.

I have received love letters in my life. All the same, I have never comprehended a love message as remotely wonderful and beautiful as God's Holy written Word. Today, my heart is still full and still smiles when meditating upon Him. To thoroughly understand God's purpose for my life, as it is with those who accept His Son, Jesus, as Lord and Savior, is most definitely a life-changing experience. It is such a blessing to designate time to become knowledgeable of Jehovah's love. Additionally, to make a determination to follow Jesus, altogether, solidified me in God, gave me victory over sin, and empowered me with ever-lasting joy. Categorically, joyfulness is a stimulant to strength.

I am reminded of a time when I called upon the name of my omnipotent Father after experiencing the most horrendous slip and fall ever. My footing was lost before, but this particular occasion was unforgettable. The floor mat was removed from the entranceway of the shower to be added to the wash; however, I did not notice that a replacement mat was never placed before entering the shower. As I proceeded out of the shower, I continued onto the floor. Stepping out the shower, ending up on the floor, and not recollecting anything momentarily was horrifying. My husband was in the master suite relaxing in bed, he heard the commotion and darted into the master bathroom within what appeared to be a fraction of a second. As he assisted me up, I comprehended I had no feeling in my legs. Literally, my legs were immobile; therefore, standing was impossible at that time. My hands were numb and tingling tremendously and I become discombobulated; as a result, fathoming a comprehension of exactly what transpired took a while.

Accordingly, my husband had to drag me, drenching wet, into the bedroom. He tried for several minutes to get me onto the bed. Finally, I suggested for him to get onto the bed and pull me back as close to the bed as he could, then interlock his arms in mine from my backside to lift me up while I pressed myself tightly to the bed between pauses. Of course, prayer was going forth throughout the ordeal. He eventually got me onto the bed. I was one happy sister!

My hands and legs suffered severe nerve damage. I tried moving my fingers, toes, and legs, but it was unmanageable. I knew if I wanted to become mobile again, trusting in my Father was the only way. As much as my husband loved me, he could not help me aside from praying for me, which he perpetually did. Subsequent trying to force my toes and fingers to move after what seemed to be hours, a couple of my fingers moved minimally. My enthusiasm lengthened, and, over a process of time, more fingers moved and my toes and legs became strengthened. Ultimately, my husband would periodically assist me to my feet until I was able to take a step; he repeated this methodology until ambulation was possible.

Although I moved slowly, however, I gave God praise and thanksgiving for blessing me. I witnessed the omnipotence of God, an all-powerful God who rescued me once again from the clutches of the enemy, who, by the way, tried to convince me that I would be crippled. Still, the Devil is a lying wonder.

My unshakeable faith in my Father caused me to concentrate upon Him and His promises. He is omnipotent and nothing is too difficult for Him. When I became strong enough, my husband took me to the hospital, and after numerous examinations, the physician determined I strained my back, which he and a chiropractor diagnosed as cervical stenosis in my back. As far as mobility, I am not one hundred percent back; nevertheless, I am mobile and I give God the praise. God is a good God! He never failed me; neither did He ever forsake me. He is an omnipresent Father who is everywhere I am. God, I thank you for your love and protection, and your omniscience, omnipotence, and omnipresence.

The Openhandedness of Our Father
CHAPTER 11

The goodness and kindness of God is never-ending; He is inclined in showering down His favor upon His children's lives. When it feels like there is no way out of your difficulties, it is God's amazing grace that sees you through. When you do not know what to speak, it is through His omniscience in which you speak. When your circumstances have you feeling pessimistic to the point that you feel doomed, it is your Father's love and comfort that gives you peace throughout your life's storms. When you are experiencing hopelessness, it is through God's anointing that you are bursting with purpose.

If your spirit is discouraged, meditate upon the Holy Word of God and become encouraged. If it appears your strength is disintegrating from within you, stir up the gift of praise, so joy might stream through you. If your marriage is on unsteady ground, rebuke the Devil and he will not hang around. If you desire to hear from God, get in a quiet place, listen for His voice, and receive a rhema (anointed, life changing) word. If you need spiritual intelligence, seek God's wisdom, for it is the principle thing to do. If you are medically ill, trust in the healing virtue of Jesus. If you have sinned, God is forgiving; He will rehabilitate you. If you have fallen and find it troublesome to pick back up, the outstretched hand of God will assist you onto your feet.

If you backslid from your spiritual conviction, God will reinstate your salvation, refurbish your faith, reintroduce your joy, and redecorate your spirit. So, why don't you experience the openhandedness of God? Reach out and receive His ever-present help.

"And I will make them and the places round about my hill a blessing; and I will cause the shower to come down in his season; there shall be showers of blessing." (Ezekiel 34:26, KJV)

God our Father is a wonderful guiding light that shines upon us to give us direction and protection. He provisions us with refinement and glory, and He promises to never withhold His goodness from anyone that demonstrates uprightness. Therefore, I encourage everyone to allow God's glory to shine during the course of your life, and He will singlehandedly, openhandedly, and enthusiastically outpour abundant blessings throughout your life for functioning within the spirit of conformism.

Ask, and It Shall Be Given You! Seek and You Shall Find!

Now that we comprehend the bountifulness of God, we should be confident that God unstintingly gives a bestowment of necessities, gifts, handouts, conversions, and other benedictions to saints and non-saints. In all things, whatsoever ye shall ask in prayer believing, God promises to give munificently. If your marriage needs to be consecrated back to God, if you require physical restoration, or if you need peacetime, ask and it shall be given. For illustration, if your marriage is deficient in affection, admiration, and sanctification, God is able to bring these dead components back to life. Christians should not live in disunification. Disunification is the destruction of unity and harmony within what should be an otherwise sanctified and dedicated union before God. At times, even as Saints of God, the Devil ambuscades our marriages, causing quarrels between husbands and wives. When the Devil dispatches his demons throughout marriages, spouses become most disrespectful, thus weakening the admiration they once reciprocated toward each other.

Consequently, once shared love and affection disintegrate, couples begin falling out of love, and then the Devil starts laughing at them as they crumble. God established the church after the family. Good behaviors, peaceful encounters, pleasant conversations, and positive mindsets should be predominant concerning how husbands and wives look at each other. Viewing the husband as handsome and recognizing the wife as beautiful is still necessary within marriages. Therefore, Christians should take their families back from Satan by sanctifying themselves from wickedness, for instance, husbands slapping wives if they are not obedient and if dinner is not on the table when they get in from work, if the children are too loud, or simply because they had a bad day at work. Additionally, some wives belittle their husbands for being inadequate performers in comparison to other men. I assure you, Saints of God, these characteristics are unacceptable and not pleasing before God. Such Christians must comprehend that they make spectacles of themselves before their counterparts.

This is why, sanctification is imperative. This can be done through distinguishing which spirit is in operation every time you and your family members interact. Humbling yourselves before the all mighty God is what must be done for these types of households to experience decontamination. Just call upon Jehovah-Maccaddeshem, the God that specializes in sanctification. Purification might be received through prophecies. God encourage saints to not despise prophecies. As an ordained prophetess, I have counseled numerous married couples; speaking as the oracle of God is paramount in bringing rehabilitation to troubled marriages. Rehabilitation reestablishes goodness within the hearts and spirits of Christian families, providing them with indispensable tools that empower them to withdraw from all appearances of evil. This opens a pathway for the God of peace to completely consecrate and consummate the family unto Him so families become trained through the anointing in how to effectively exchange affection, admiration, and respectful conversation between each other.

In addition, Ephesians 5:22-26 reminds Christian wives that the high priest or headship within their marriage is their own husband in the same way as Christ is Savior and headship of the church, which is the body of Christ. Hence, as the church—the body of Christ—is subject and submissive unto Christ, Christian wives should also be to their husbands in everything. The Bible instructs husbands to love their wives as Christ also loves the church and gave himself for it. Christ was willing to give His life so that He might bring sanctification and purification to it through the washing of water through God's Word (KJV). Moreover, the Bible explicated that this was accomplished so Jesus might present the church to Himself as a glorious church, without spot or wrinkle, and free of contamination (Ephesians 5:27 KJV). Therefore, husbands should love their wives as they do their own bodies. For the Word of God says, he that loves his wife loves himself (Ephesians 5:28 KJV). Husbands, to love your wives as Christ loves the church means you must nourish her and cherish her.

If you are unhealthy because of an illness or medical condition, you need to get in touch with Jehovah Rapha, for he is the God who heals. Matthew 9:32-35 discusses the parable of the dumb speechless man who was demon possessed. The Bible says when God caste the dumb devil out of the man, he then spoke and a multitude of Israelites marveled because the nation never witnessed such miracle. Subsequently, the Pharisees said, "He casts out demons by the ruler of the demons" (Matthew 9:34

NKJV). That parable, however, further explains how Jesus journeyed throughout every city and village, teaching and preaching within their synagogues the gospel of the kingdom of Heaven, healing and delivering every sickness and every disease that bound those societies (see Mathew 9:35 KJV).

Healing is for everyone. He saw the multitudes and He was moved with compassion for them, because they were weary and scattered, like sheep having no shepherd (Mathew 9:36 NKJV). In addition, Exodus 15:26 states Jehovah Rapha, the healer, will deliver us from the demon of infirmity, for sickness comes from Satan. Saints can circumvent sicknesses by diligently hearkening to the voice of the Lord our God, by willingly doing that which is suitable, tolerable, and honorable within His sight, by meticulously giving our undivided attention to His commandments, and by fastidiously keeping all His statutes. He promised to never permit any manner of infections or diseases to overtake us like those He commissioned to come upon the Egyptians because of the imbalanced relationship between them and God.

Moreover, Luke 4:18 (KJV) expounds, "The Spirit of the Lord is upon me, because he hath anointed me to preach the gospel to the poor; he hath sent me to heal the brokenhearted, to preach deliverance to the captives, and recovering of sight to the blind, to set at liberty them that are bruised."

If your life lacks coherence, Jehovah Shalom is the Lord of Peace. Philippians 4:4-9 KJV is self-explanatory and extraordinary in encouraging saints of God:

> Rejoice in the Lord always: and again I say, Rejoice. Let your moderation be known unto all men. The Lord is at hand. Be careful for nothing; but in everything by prayer and supplication with thanksgiving let your requests be made known unto God. And the peace of God, which passeth all understanding, shall keep your hearts and minds through Christ Jesus. Finally, brethren, whatsoever things are true, whatsoever things are honest, whatsoever things are just, whatsoever things are pure, whatsoever things are lovely, whatsoever things are of good report; if there be any virtue, and if there be any praise, think on these things. Those things, which ye have both learned, and received, and heard, and seen in me, do: and the God of peace shall be with you.

Remember Jehovah Jireh is the God who provides and presents you with whatever it is you need. Throughout the Bible, there are beyond twenty matchless names of God documented. Whenever you are praying for yourself, other Christians, or the world at large, call Him by the suitable name. This enables you to become knowledgeable of Him in different lights. Likewise, numerous names of God are listed below to assist you throughout your investigation and education concerning Him.

The Matchless Names of God

Yahweh-Shammah or Adonai-Shammah: *God as lordship and master*

Malachi 1:6:

> A son honors his father and a servant honors his master. Therefore, if I be your Father, where is mine honor? And, if I be your Master, where is my fear? This says the Lord of hosts unto you. O ecclesiastics that loathe my name. And, next you ask, in what capacity have we despised thy name?

God is a Holy and divine being with authority, governance, and influence over individuals, especially His children.

Jehovah Jireh: *The Lord who provides*
Genesis 22:13-14:

> Abraham looked up, and behold, stood behind him was a ram caught in a thicket by his horns: and Abraham went and took the ram, and offered him up for a burnt offering in the stead of his son. And Abraham called the name of that place Jehovahjireh: as it is said to this day, in the mount of the Lord it shall be seen

God provides you with both your needs and your desires. Therefore, do not hesitate to make your requests, and watch Him fulfill His Word throughout your life.

Jehovah-Maccaddeshem: *The Lord, your sanctifier*

Exodus 31:13: "Speak to the children of Israel; tell them, to keep my sabbaths for, it is a sign between me and you throughout your generations, that you might know that I am the Lord that sanctifies you."

Our Father consecrates us through Holy dedications unto Himself, so that we might be the epitome of holiness.

Yahweh: *The Lord*

Genesis 2:4: "These are the generations of the heavens and of the earth when they were created, in the day that the Lord God made the earth and the heavens."

The Lord God formed heaven and earth, assorted waters, varied plants and diversified fruit trees, individuals and animals, gold medals and miscellaneous stones, and everything within this life. We are His craftsmanship, fearfully and wonderfully fashioned. For, the Lord is our God.

Jehovah Shammah: *The Lord is always present*

Deuteronomy 31:6: "Be strong and of a good courage, fear not, neither become fearful of them: for the Lord your God is He that goes with you; He will never fail you, neither will He abandon (forsake) you."

The Lord is always available when you need Him, and He will always make sure you are victorious in all you attempt. Trust Him and never become fearful-thinking that He is not present.

Jehovah Nissi: *The Lord, my banner*

He brought me to the banqueting house, and his banner over me was love.

The Lord God, who is love, blesses His children with sup (the Bread of Life), in the spirit of love. The Word of God is both delicious and nutritious. The banner of God's light shines on both sides of us and above our heads. This glory of God symbolizes Christians' transformations and categorizations as children of God.

Jehovah-Raah or Jehovah Rohi: *The Lord, my shepherd*
Psalm 23:1-6:

> The Lord is my shepherd; I shall not want. He maketh me to lie down in green pastures: he leadeth me beside the still waters. He restoreth my soul: he leadeth me in the paths of righteousness for his name's sake. Yea, though I walk through the valley of the shadow of death, I will fear no evil: for thou art with me; thy rod and thy staff they comfort me. Thou preparest a table before me in the

presence of mine enemies: thou anointest my head with oil; my cup runneth over. Surely goodness and mercy shall follow me all the days of my life: and I will dwell in the house of the Lord forever.

We do not have to want for anything; our needs are met through God's promises. They are ours for the asking and God's for the giving. Always know God safeguards us from evil, and blesses us with an overflow of bestowments in the presence of our enemies.

Jehovah Tsidkenu: *The Lord, our righteousness*

Jeremiah 23:6: "In his days Judah shall be saved, and Israel shall dwell safely: and this is his name whereby he shall be called, 'The Lord Our Righteousness.'"

1 John 3:7: "Little children, make sure no one deceives you; the one who practices righteousness is righteous, just as He is righteous."

Jehovah Tsidkenu is our Lord, the righteousness. Therefore, we should never allow the Devil to bamboozle us to perform less than righteously, for we must demonstrate righteousness because our Father is righteous.

Jehovah Rapha: *The Lord that heals*

Leviticus 15:26 (KJV): "Each bed whereon she sitteth or lieth throughout the timespan of her issue shall be unto her as the bed of her separation: and whatsoever she sitteth upon shall be unsanitary, as the unsanitariness of her separation."

"Every bed and loveseat she lies upon during the days of her contamination will be liken unto her bed throughout the duration of her menstrual uncleanness, and any equipment and furniture she sits upon will be as contaminated as her menstruation or menstrual cycle" (HCSB).

Regardless of your bed of affliction, know that venereal diseases, viruses, and syndromes are from the Devil. God does not contaminate His children; consequently, He heals them from impurities that the adversary perpetrates against them physiologically. So, trust Jehovah Rapha—the Lord that Heals—to decontaminate your body.

Jehovah Shalom: *The Lord is peace*

Judges 6:23-24: "And the Lord said unto him, 'Peace be unto thee; fear not: thou shalt not die. Then Gideon built an altar there unto the Lord, and called it Jehovah shalom: unto this day it is yet in Ophrah of the Abiezrites."

Philippians 4:7: "And the peace of God, which passeth all understanding, shall keep your hearts and minds through Christ Jesus."

To circumvent troubled hearts and disturbed minds, Christians must recollect the fact that we have the mind of Christ; therefore, we should always consent to have God's peace permeate our every thought through concentrating upon His powerful, yet peaceful, Word. God is His Word, and He is Jehovah Shalom, the God of peace. He knows how to keep His children psychologically and spiritually undisturbed. He is our rock, and it is through His spirit that we are comforted. If Christians remain reconciled mentally and conceptually with Christ Jesus, this gives us understanding that without such reconciliation, our comprehension would remain clouded or annulled altogether. So, relax your minds, trust your Father, and watch Him smooth out your circumstances!

Jehovah Sabaoth: *The Lord of Hosts*

Isaiah 6:1-3 (KJV):

> In the year that king Uzziah died I saw also the Lord sitting upon a throne, high and lifted up, and his train filled the temple. Above it stood the seraphims: each one had six wings; with twain he covered his face, and with twain he covered his feet, and with twain he did fly. And one cried unto another, and said, "Holy, holy, holy, is the Lord of hosts: the whole earth is full of his glory."

El Elohim: *All-powerful Creator*

Genesis 1:1: "In the beginning (El Elohim) created the heaven and the earth."

God is maker and creator of all things existent.

El Shaddai: *The Lord God Almighty*

Genesis 17:1: "And when Abram was ninety years old and nine, the Lord appeared to Abram, and said unto him, 'I am the Almighty God; walk before me, and be thou perfect.'"

Genesis 49:25 (AMP): "God of your father who will assist you, it is the Almighty who blesses you with blessings from the heavens above. His blesses rain from the deepest to the highest places. His blessings flow throughout (nursing) breasts and (producing) wombs."

Psalm 91:1: "He that dwelleth in the secret place of the Most High shall abide under the shadow of the Almighty."

El Elyon: *The Highest or Most High God*
Genesis 14:17-20:

> And the king of Sodom went out to meet him after his return from the slaughter of Chedorlaomer, and of the kings that were with him, at the valley of Shaveh, which is the king's dale. And Melchizedek, King of Salem brought forth bread and wine: and he was the priest of the highest God. And he blessed him, and said, "Blessed be Abram of the most high God, possessor of heaven and earth: And blessed be the most high God, which hath delivered thine enemies into thy hand." And he gave him tithes of all.

El Olam: *The Everlasting God*

Isaiah 40:28-31:

> Hast thou not known? Hast thou not heard, that the everlasting God, the Lord, the Creator of the ends of the earth, fainteth not, neither is weary? There is no searching of his understanding. He giveth power to the faint; and to them that have no might he increaseth strength. Even the youths shall faint and be weary, and the young men shall utterly fall: But they that wait upon the Lord shall renew their strength; they shall mount up with wings as eagles; they shall run, and not be weary; and they shall walk, and not faint.

(In-text citation for the Matchless Names of God: Blue Letter Bible, 2017)

Remember that God is a Matchless Confidante

Whichever one of His names you choose to acknowledge Him as when praying, always know He promised to come to your rescue and drive out every hindering cause in your life. No weapon formulated against you will prosper (Isaiah 54:17).

Take a praise break; you are victorious!

Your Soul's Desires: Let Us Pray

Let us always pray without wavering

Let us always pray with a forgiving spirit

Let us always pray God's living word

Let us always pray in the name of Jesus

Let us always pray for the world at large

Let us always pray without discontinuation

Let us always pray within the spirit of love

Let us always pray with all earnestness

Children of God, let us always pray!

~ Blondie Williams ~

Psalm 37:4-5 says to "delight yourself in the Lord, and He will give you the desires of your heart. Commit thy way unto the Lord; trust also in him; and he shall bring it to pass" (KJV). Our heart's desires influence us to accomplish immeasurable things. Therefore, we must make certain that our hungers and thirsts come from God. Only He can make available those unquenchable essentials. He encourages us to come before His throne with boldness, assurance, and a spirit of forgiveness and compassion toward others. Our desires must be in conformity with His will. As Christians, we know the will of God is the Living Word of God. Therefore, when our desires and visualizations fall within alignment with Jehovah Jireh's (the God who provides) strategies, then God will unleash those blessings.

Remember, you are prayer warriors, and a prevailing
prayer life is an orthodoxy that keeps you strong, keeps
you close to God, and keeps your needs met
~ Blondie Williams ~

A Prayerful and Faithful Soul

CHAPTER 12

*F*ret not thyself because of evildoers, neither be thou envious against the workers of iniquity. For they shall soon be cut down like the grass, and wither as the green herb. Trust in the Lord, and do good; so shalt thou dwell in the land, and verily thou shalt be fed. Delight thyself also in the Lord: and he shall give thee the desires of thine heart. Commit thy way unto the Lord; trust also in him; and he shall bring it to pass. And he shall bring forth thy righteousness as the light, and thy judgment as the noonday. Rest in the Lord, and wait patiently for him: fret not thyself because of him who prospereth in his way, because of the man who bringeth wicked devices to pass. Cease from anger, and forsake wrath: fret not thyself in any wise to do evil. (Psalm 37:1-8 KJV)

God is a giving God. He wants us to have whatsoever we desire. We must understand that we have a responsibility to be faithful to His promises. It is important that we keep God at the forefront of our lives to procure our desires. God's spirit is generous. So, we must remain faithful to avoid backsliding to our previous sinful lifestyles and developing reprobate minds. Remember that everyone who sins hates God. So, keep the Devil underneath your feet and continue marching forward.

Remain Faithful to God

F = Fervent in prayer

A = Abhor immorality and cleave to morality

I = In alignment with the Word of God

T = Trust and never doubt

H = Humbleness of heart and calmness of spirit

F = Fret not yourselves because of wrongdoers

U = Unadulterated conversations and performances

L = Love without hypocrisy

By Blondie Morris Williams

"Christians who are faithful within the least extent are faithful within the greatest extent, and individuals who are unjust within the least capacity are unjust within the greatest capacity" (Luke 16:10 KJV).

"Saints of God, love God forever, for our Father preserves the faithful, and He bountifully rewards worshippers with superior attitudes and prideful and praiseful spirits" (Psalm 31:23 KJV).

Highway Infrastructure: A Bridge Leading into God's Kingdom: Introducing and Interconnecting Sinners to Christ

CHAPTER 13

*I*f anyone reading this book is not a Christian, there is an opportunity for you to discontinue traveling the downward roadway that leads to hell and become redirected by God's love to travel the pathway that guarantees you an everlasting home in God's kingdom, which is heaven. To experience this amazing life is to be transformed and to become led through the authority of God's spirit, becoming completely secure within Him. Salvation is free. Before the foundation of the world, Jesus' divine kingdom was predetermined and God utilized prophets to prognosticate or prophecy that He would buy back humankind through Jesus, sacrificing His life. Through doing so, the existing kingdom of heaven was established through the indwelling of the Holy Ghost to empower individuals with the capability to demonstrate attitudes, behaviors, and appearances that cause the light of God to shine from within them and throughout their lives.

So, let God's kingdom come into your hearts and enter into His everlasting joy!

To Become an Ambassador for God's Kingdom, Humbly Pray:

Father God, I am a sinner and I am in need of a personal Savior. I confess to you that I live a sin-filled lifestyle and I realize that without a relationship with you, through accepting Jesus, I am lost. Therefore, I pray you transform my mind, heart, spirit, soul, and body through the power of your spirit, so I may live a God-filled lifestyle and teach others to do the same. Make me over and live within me, Lord. Fill me with your Holy Spirit. I need your anointing to assist me with reading and studying the Word of God, and maintaining a Christian standard of living. God, I confess with my mouth that I am a born again Christian forever!

Welcome to the Family of God!

Spiritual Nourishment and Encouragement

As you begin your Christian journey, should you experience paralysis in spiritual growth, feel as though you are suffering an eviction of peace and joy, or develop a lack of encouragement, or a different type of difficulty or adversity, spiritual nourishment (The Word of God) will minister to those places of debilitation and deliver you from such impositions (In Touch Ministries, 2016). Remember, God is always concerned about everything that concerns you and involves you. He gave us His Word, which is His love to comfort you, strengthen you, and preserve you within His kingdom. Therefore, in faith, always speak God's word in every circumstance and it will began recharging, refilling, and renewing you through His anointing. Eating nourishment from various food groups is responsible for the breakdown of nutrition into fats, healthy carbohydrates, high proteins, and multivitamins and minerals that travel throughout your digestive system and stimulate you with physical is what is recommended to maintain life. Similarly, spiritual nourishment is a requirement to maintaining spiritual strength, health, and life in Christ. God's Word conducts spiritual reconstruction and spiritual maintenance to every component of your life that becomes weakened or broken. Additionally, if you encounter sickness throughout your Christian journey, spiritual nourishment is exceptional in ministering to your personal need and, in turn, causes you to experience wellness psychologically, physiologically, or spiritually.

Therefore, reading from Matthew to Revelation everyday will prevent you, as a Christian, from ever experiencing spiritual malnutrition. Every book of the Bible provides spiritual information, direction, encouragement, and empowerment, as required, to say the least. Christians must maintain solidification in God, and being well fed upon His Word keeps you spiritually awakened. Spiritual awareness is astronomical in remaining watchful, prayerful, and always abounding within God's Word. So, feast off God's nourishment and remain spiritually healthy and pleasurably contented. As this meal becomes settled within your spirit and demonstrated throughout your life, your spiritual influence and intelligence become more sharpened and your relationship with God becomes more rock-solid. Then you will be able to advocate that you are: "Solidified in God, the Devil is defeated."

Avoid Psychological and Physiological Burnout throughout
Your New Life in Christ

As Christians, serving God is a marvelous standard of living. Our lifestyles embroil numerous involvements from brother- hood, sisterhood, and priesthood to fatherhood, motherhood, and conjugal-hood. Conceivably, we could become physio- logically exhausted at some point within our journey of life attending weekly spiritual and nonspiritual engagements. For this reason, we must make certain that we do not overload our schedules otherwise we would burn ourselves out. A burnout is synonymous to a breakdown. A breakdown is emotional or physiological exhaustion that results from a combination of environmental conditions, external stimuluses, or internal stressors. Correspondingly, individuals experiencing burnout showcase a progressively negative attitude toward their occupa- tions, have low self-esteem, and personally devalue themselves. It is paramount that strategies for circumventing and handling breakdown embrace utilization of assertive methodologies, expansion of decision-making and problem-solving conceptu- alizations, clarification of personal standardizations, and imple- mentation of both reasonable and attainable individualistic objectives. Notwithstanding, comprehending and implementing coping mechanisms to assist us with advantageously managing our emotions; scheduling acceptable recreation, relaxation, and restoration involvements; and diminishing stressors within our work life and home life is mandatory if we, as Christians, are to live well-adjusted existences (Burnout, n.d.).

Empowering Scriptures
Meditate Upon God Day and Night

Matthew 5:43-45 KJV

Ye have heard that it hath been said, Thou shalt love thy neighbour, and hate thine enemy. But I say unto you, love your enemies, bless them that curse you, do good to them that hate you, and pray for them which despitefully use you, and persecute you; That ye may be the children of your Father which is in heaven: for he maketh his sun to rise on the evil and on the good, and sendeth rain on the just and on the unjust.

1 Corinthians 13:1-3 KJV

Though I speak with the tongues of men and of angels, and have not charity, I am become as sounding brass, or a tinkling cymbal. And though I have the gift of prophecy, and understand all mysteries, and all knowledge; and though I have all faith, so that I could remove mountains, and have not charity, I am nothing. And though I bestow all my goods to feed the poor, and though I give my body to be burned, and have not charity, it profiteth me nothing.

Deuteronomy 31:6 KJV

Be strong and of a good courage, fear not, nor be afraid of them: for the Lord thy God, he it is that doth go with thee; he will not fail thee, nor forsake thee.

Romans 10:15 TLB

And how will anyone go and tell them unless someone sends him? That is what the Scriptures are talking about when they say, "How beautiful are the feet of those who preach the Gospel of peace with God and bring glad tidings of good things." In other words, how welcome are those who come preaching God's Good News!

Joshua 1:9 KJV

Have not I commanded thee? Be strong and of a good courage; be not afraid, neither be thou dismayed: for the Lord thy God is with thee whithersoever thou goest.

2 Samuel 14:17 TLB

Yes, the king will give us peace again. I know that you are like an angel of God and can discern good from evil. May God be with you.

Psalm 18:2 KJV

The Lord is my rock, and my fortress, and my deliverer; my God, my strength, in whom I will trust; my buckler, and the horn of my salvation, and my high tower.

Philippians 4:7 TLB

You will experience God's peace, which is far more wonderful than the human mind can understand. His peace will keep your thoughts and your hearts quiet and at rest as you trust in Christ Jesus.

Psalm 19:14 KJV

Let the words of my mouth, and the meditation of my heart, be acceptable in thy sight, O Lord, my strength, and my redeemer.

Psalm 28:7 KJV

The Lord is my strength and my shield; my heart trusted in him, and I am helped: therefore my heart greatly rejoiceth; and with my song will I praise him."

Romans 8:26 KJV

Likewise the Spirit also helpeth our infirmities: for we know not what we should pray for as we ought: but the Spirit itself maketh intercession for us with groanings which cannot be uttered."

Psalm 150 KJV

Praise ye the Lord. Praise God in his sanctuary: praise him in the firmament of his power. Praise him for his mighty acts: praise him according to his excellent greatness.Praise him with the sound of the trumpet: praise him with the psaltery and harp. Praise him with the timbrel and dance: praise him with stringed instruments and organs. Praise him upon the loud cymbals: praise him upon the high sounding cymbals. Let every thing that hath breath praise the Lord. Praise ye the Lord.

Philippians 4:4 KJV

Rejoice in the Lord always: and again I say, rejoice.

Matthew 5:9 TLB

Happy are those who strive for peace, they shall be called the sons of God.

Romans 5:1 TLB

So now, since we have been made right in God's sight by faith in his promises, we can have real peace with him because of what Jesus Christ our Lord has done for us.

Ephesians 1:3-4

Blessed be the God and Father of our Lord Jesus Christ, who hath blessed us with all spiritual blessings in heavenly places in Christ: According as he hath chosen us in him before the foundation of the world, that we should be holy and without blame before him in love.

Psalm 27:1 KJV

The Lord is my light and my salvation; whom shall I fear? The Lord is the strength of my life; of whom shall I be afraid?

Psalm 28:7 KJV

The Lord is my strength and my shield; my heart trusted in him, and I am helped: therefore my heart greatly rejoiceth; and with my song will I praise him.

Jude 1:2 TLB

May you be given more and more of God's kindness, peace, and love.

Acts 10:36-37 TLB

I'm sure you have heard about the Good News for the people of Israel—that there is peace with God through Jesus, the Messiah, who is Lord of all creation. This message has spread all through Judea, beginning with John the Baptist in Galilee.

Isaiah 52:7 TLB

How beautiful upon the mountains are the feet of those who bring the happy news of peace and salvation, the news that the God of Israel reigns.

James 1:2-4 KJV

My brethren, count it all joy when ye fall into divers temptations; Knowing this, that the trying of your faith worketh patience. But let patience have her perfect work, that ye may be perfect and entire, wanting nothing.

Romans 15:4 KJV

For whatsoever things were written aforetime were written for our learning, that we through patience and comfort of the scriptures might have hope.

Hebrews 4:16 KJV

Let us therefore come boldly unto the throne of grace that we may obtain mercy, and find grace to help in time of need.

John 4:24 AMP

God is spirit [the Source of life, yet invisible to mankind], and those who worship Him must worship in spirit and truth.

Galatians 6:1 KJV

Brethren, if a man be overtaken in a fault, ye which are spiritual, restore such a one in the spirit of meekness; considering thyself, lest thou also be tempted.

Romans 6:8 KJV

For to be carnally minded is death; but to be spiritually minded is life and peace. Because the carnal mind is enmity against God: for it is not subject to the law of God, neither indeed can be. So then they that are in the flesh cannot please God.

Deuteronomy 11:1 AMP

[Rewards of Obedience] Therefore you shall love the Lord your God, and always keep His charge, His statutes, His precepts, and His commandments [it is your obligation to Him].

Acts 1:8 KJV

But ye shall receive power, after that the Holy Ghost is come upon you: and ye shall be witnesses unto me both in Jerusalem, and in all Judaea, and in Samaria, and unto the uttermost part of the earth.

Romans 1:16 KJV

For I am not ashamed of the gospel of Christ: for it is the power of God unto salvation to everyone that believeth; to the Jew first, and also to the Greek.

Romans 3:38:39 KJV

For I am persuaded, that neither death, nor life, nor angels, nor principalities, nor powers, nor things present, nor things to come, Nor height, nor depth, nor any other creature, shall be able to separate us from the love of God, which is in Christ Jesus our Lord.

Galatians 5:6 KJV

For in Jesus Christ neither circumcision avails anything, nor uncircumcision; but faith which works by love.

Mark 9:50 KJV

Salt is good: but if the salt has lost his saltiness, wherewith will ye season it? Have salt in yourselves, and have peace one with another.

Romans 8:35-37 KJV

Who shall separate us from the love of Christ? Shall tribulation, or distress, or persecution, or famine, or nakedness, or peril, or sword? As it is written, for thy sake we are killed all the day long; we are accounted as sheep for the slaughter. Nay, in all these things we are more than conquerors through him that loved us.

Luke 10:27 KJV

And he answering said Thou shalt love the Lord thy God with all thy heart, and with all thy soul, and with all thy strength, and with all thy mind; and thy neighbour as thyself.

Galatians 5:1 KJV

Stand fast therefore in the liberty wherewith Christ hath made us free, and be not entangled again with the yoke of bondage.

Ephesians 4:2-3 KJV

With all lowliness and meekness, with longsuffering forbearing one another in love; Endeavoring to keep the unity of the Spirit in the bond of peace.

Psalm 121:1-3 KJV

I will lift up mine eyes unto the hills, from whence cometh my help. My help comes from the Lord, which made heaven and earth. He will not suffer thy foot to be moved: he that keeps thee will not slumber.

2 Corinthians 13:11 TLB

I close my letter with these last words: Be happy. Grow in Christ. Pay attention to what I have said. Live in harmony and peace. And may the God of love and peace be with you.

Notations

Notations

Notations

Notations

Works Cited

Blue Letter Bible, 2017. *The Names of God in the Old Testament* Retrieved July 3, 2017, from https://www.blueletterbible. org/study/misc/name_god.cfm

Burnout. (n.d.) *Miller-Keane Encyclopedia and Dictionary of Medicine, Nursing, and Allied Health, Seventh Edition.* (2003). Retrieved October 9 2016 from http://medical_dictionary. thefreedictionary.com/burnout

Deffinbaugh, B. (2017). Taking a Second Look at Submission (1 Peter 2:13-3:7). Retrieved July 3, 2017, from https:// bible.org/seriespage/15-taking-second-look-submission-1-peter-213-37

Merriam-Webster. (2017). https://www.merriam-webster.com/

Temple, T. (n.d.). *God's complete knowledge.* Retrieved from http://www.livingbiblestudies.org/study/TT45/007.html

What does it mean that God is omnipresent? Retrieved from https://www.gotquestions.org/God-omnipresent.html

Whelchel, H. (2017). *For principles of Biblical stewardship.* Retrieved from https://tifwe.org/four-principles-of-biblicle-stewardship/

Zalta, E. N., Hoffman, J & Rosenkrantz, G. (2014) *Omnipotence.* The Stanford Encyclopedia of Philosophy (Spring 2012 Edition). Retrieved from http://plato.stanford.edu/archives/spr2012/entries/omnipotence/

About the Author

Blondie Y. Williams is a resident of Covington, Georgia. She is an author, prophetess, and pastor. Her pastorship is an ordained online ministry. Through teaching and reaching individuals beyond the walls of a local church is necessary. Christian's are to preach the Gospel of Jesus throughout the world. Therefore, through Internet mediums, millions of individuals have immediate accessibility to the word of God anywhere in the world simultaneously. Overall, this methodology is highly contributory in enlarging the kingdom of God.

Pastor Williams enjoys accumulating intelligence. She attended seven pedagogical institutions and received eight collegiate documentations. Six, however, were accomplished with honorary commendations with GPAs ranging from 3.71 to 4.0. Pastor Williams earned educational qualifications exemplify:

undergraduate and graduate certificates, (1) diploma, (2) AAS, (1) BSBA, (1) MBA, (1) MS, and she has a few more years outstanding before she accomplishes her DBA scholarship. Additionally, Pastor Williams is contemporaneously an alumnus and student at Columbia Southern University, and a member of several honor societies; notwithstanding, her grandest achievement in life is becoming an ordained child of God.

CPSIA information can be obtained
at www.ICGtesting.com
Printed in the USA
LVOW05s2319050318
568809LV00011B/1075/P